"Seeking Good - Attracting Evil"
A Minister's Shocking Story

Robert (Bob) Jennings

Seeking Good - Attracting Evil
A Minister's Shocking Story

All Rights Reserved
Copyright © 2025 by Robert (Bob) Jennings

Paperback ISBN: 9798999180803
Ebook ISBN: 9798999180834

Unless otherwise indicated.
Scripture quotations taken from the New King James Version (NKJV).

Copyright 1982 by Thomas Nelson, Inc.
Used by permission.

Author contact information:
Email – bob@seekinggoodattractingevil.com

Websites:
seekinggoodattractingevil2.com
seekinggoodattractingevil.com
wdmbooks.org

SGAE Enterprise
P.O. Box 445
Perris, CA 92572-0445

Table of Contents

"Seeking Good - Attracting Evil" 1
A Minister's Shocking Story 1
Publisher/Copyright/AuthorInfo 2
Introduction 5
Credits & Acknowledgments 7
    Chapter 1 8
My Three Blunders as A Kid 8
    Chapter 2 11
The Work Ethic – My Formative Years 11
    Chapter 3 18
Some Awards in Athletics and Other Reflections 18
    Chapter 4 23
Experience in Mexico 23
    Chapter 5 29
Meeting Some Celebrities 29
    Chapter 6 34
Finding What was Missing 34
    Chapter 7 39
Early Ministry Experiences 39
    Chapter 8 43
Biblical Training, Marriage, and Work 43
    Chapter 9 50
A New Opportunity – A New Direction 50
    Chapter 10 65
A Peep at Home Life 65
    Chapter 11 67
What's with Our Funding? 67
    Chapter 12 72
A New Company 72
    Chapter 13 75
The Infamous Gold Deal and Coal Venture 75

Chapter 14	84
Company Collapse - That Fateful Day	84
Chapter 15	93
Incarceration in Arizona	93
Chapter 16	98
Incarceration in Texas	98
Chapter 17	105
From La Tuna to Mendota	105
Chapter 18	110
Early Days at Camp Mendota	110
Chapter 19	119
Moving Through the Years	119
Chapter 20	131
The City of Light	131
Chapter 21	138
The Straight Talk Program	138
Chapter 22	143
The Downside and Upside	143
Chapter 23	154
God at Work - What About the Great Commission?	154
Chapter 24	164
What Now?	164
Epilogue	170
Exhibits:	178
The Believer's Prison Creed	184
Reference Credits	185
Location Maps	186

Introduction

My book is about the life of an ordinary kid growing to adulthood in South Central Los Angeles. My father instilled in me the virtue of a good work ethic, which I experienced growing up, and how it affected my approach to athletics and employment. This story will share the blunders and triumphs of my life, the sports accomplishments, meetings and interactions with celebrities, and international travels occurring over the course of my life. I will share my conversion experience and call to Christian ministry, my deep disappointment of a failed business venture, and loss of my case in trial, which brought 10 years of incarceration. The effect of the sentencing duration upon my family's life and mine, caused the darkest moment in our lives.

The story is an encouragement to those who have fallen as believers, and disappointed God through one's sinful decisions and actions. Those who have experienced defeat, may believe the days of being used by God have ended. The story will breathe hope into those, helping them to realize God already knew everything we would do prior to us doing them. Our God is an understanding God, who loves us, and yet will discipline us. After all our failings, He will forgive us, and extend grace and mercy to us, if we have a repentant heart. God wants to finish His work in us, and through us, going beyond what we thought would ever be possible, for His glory.

It is a story of how God caused a rebirth of ministry in prison, and the development of discipleship biblical studies to grow believers. The details of life in prison are shared. The impact my crime had on the victims is shared. This book will answer the question of where the overall church in America is today! How is the church in general, in America, doing in fulfilling the Great Commission?

My book offers biblical solutions to its fulfillment and appeals to those who have not understood God's loving provision of rescue from sin's enslavement and certain eventual punishment. Placed in the Exhibits section are certain items to assist the inquisitive reader with available discipleship growth materials. A glance of speeches made, and maps of visual locations traveled are also included.

This story will be a timely read for these last days, giving biblical perspective of the future and one's place in it. The reader will come away with why the book was entitled Seeking Good-Attracting Evil.[1]

---

[1] Proverbs 11:27

Credits & Acknowledgments

I want to extend my appreciation to God who has brought me through this journey, and to Jesus Christ who has forgiven me for all my sins and did not abandon me in spite of my failings.

I want to give special thanks to my Wife for her unyielding devotion to the Lord Jesus Christ, and steadfast love for me when it would have been easy to walk away, for all she endured and suffered during this great trial caused by me. Also thankful for my daughters' love and visits with Mom to see me, and my oldest daughter for assistance on the back-cover summary of the book.

I want to thank my Dad, Mom, and Dean for their unending devotion, visits, and financial support during my time of incarceration, and continued support in reintegration to public life. For their assistance to my wife and daughters during my incarceration, I also thank them.

I want to thank my uncle Bobby for his huge contribution to maintain a very important issue needing to be resolved.

I want to thank my cousin Linda for flying all the way to Los Angeles for my court hearing.

I want to thank my Sister and Brother-in-law for their love and support through the difficult years of incarceration. Also, for all their visits, and financial support. To my sister, thanks for her time for preliminary and closing editing of my book.

I want to thank my Brother for his love, visits, and support during incarceration, as well as his counsel and assistance in publication of my books.

I want to thank my wife's family for their financial support, to assist my wife and daughters through my years of incarceration.

I want to thank my Pastor, his wife, and church family for assistance to my wife, their support of me, and the sending of bibles for those incarcerated.

Chapter 1

My Three Blunders as A Kid

From a quiet kid, not impressive or expressive…

As a kid growing up in the south-central area of Los Angeles, I was shy and didn't develop any social skills. Both my parents worked, and I had an older sister of a few years who studied and played with her friends. My sister was very smart, and as I remember, almost received straight A's in grammar school. I remember, for a while my mother was at home when I started kindergarten. But the first day she met me halfway coming from school, I was angry at her because I knew my way home. I was quiet, but felt I knew my way from home to school and back home. I spent my time watching movie matinees once I was home, and climbing the neighbor's tree next door, which was in his front yard on the other side of the sidewalk where there was a 4-foot-wide strip of grass. He used to always tell me to come down from the tree and I would always find my way back up it, because I could see all over the neighborhood. I found myself daydreaming about what would my life be like in the future as I sat on a limb.

I remember three blunders I experienced while living on East 89th St, between Hooper and Zamora. The first happened after I was taken to a circus. It was very enjoyable with the high wire acts, the wild and tamed animal tricks, and the clown antics, which had the audience full of laughter. But what fascinated me more than anything else about this circus was a woman that did a balancing act, and eventually hung from her teeth from a rope supporting all her weight. So, when returning home, I was around the age of five or six years old and felt the urge to copy the stunt in one of my father's and mother's friend's backyard which had a rope hanging from a limb. I will never forget this experience as long as I live. I remember biting on that rope and swinging out of that tree, with the intent of imitating what I saw the stunt lady do in the circus. Well, I want you readers to know that my stunt did not turn out so well as you can imagine on your own. My two front teeth went straight out of their fixed position and my whole body went straight to the ground.

The pain and the blood terrified me, and I was yelling at the top of my voice.

My dad and mom's friend heard my cry, saw my mouth and shirt covered in blood, and ran to get a towel to try and stop the bleeding. Fortunately, my dad was home, and I was rushed to the nearest dental office.

I will never forget that the dental surgeon could not use any Novocain to deaden my pain. He told my dad with an assistant to hold me down in the dental chair and he had to extract my two front teeth. All I remember is screaming as the removals were being made. When all of this ended, I learned a monumental lesson that I will never forget. Do not try imitating anyone doing a circus act without first getting permission from your parents. The gap between my front two teeth is a continual reminder.

The second blunder happened one day when I did something wrong. My mom was going to wait until my dad got home to have him give me a spanking. So, I thought I would pack up, get me a stick, and tie my things together in a shirt to take up the life of a hobo - this was something I thought I would imitate watching a specific cartoon. I said to myself, I do not have to hang around here, I can make it on my own. I was about six years old at the time. So, I told my mom I was leaving home. I found a branch in the backyard from a tree, tied my clothes in my shirt (not all of them of course), but enough that I could carry.
My mom stepped aside, to my surprise, when I was getting ready to walk out the side door that leads out to the backyard. I poked out my little defiant chest and walked out. I headed for the gate that would lead me out into the alley. I walked past the incinerator (some of you will know what that is, and others will have to ask an elderly person).

Before I reached the halfway mark to get to the outlet for the street, my steps became shorter, and my mind began to reason - where am I going? How will I get something to eat? Where will I sleep? My shorter steps became no steps at all. I said to myself I have no money. With that thought, I did an about-face and went back home.

When I slipped back into the house, my mom just acted like she did not see me but continued doing what she was doing. When my dad came home my mom never mentioned what had happened to me regarding my behavior and actions. She did not need to. I learned that day a great lesson: I really needed my mom and dad, so I checked my behavior.

I was a few years older when the last serious blunder occurred during my childhood. A hardball baseball game was being played in the street I lived on, right outside my home. When I think back on this game it was a risky event from the start.

There were several vehicles parked by the curb on both sides of the street. Well, I am up to bat and hit the baseball solidly. The only negative was that it sailed straight into a neighbor's pickup truck's front window. Everyone fled. I was in trouble, big trouble. I realized even at an early age I was the guilty one. My parents always spoke about honesty. I mustered up the courage to go to the door of Mr. Giles to let him know I was the one who cracked his truck's windshield with the baseball from the swing of my bat.

He was sad that it happened and said he would have to speak to my father. Well, I hoped my dad did not make it home anytime soon. He arrived all too soon for me, and I had to tell him what I did before Mr. Giles stopped by. He of course was upset. So, after speaking with Mr. Giles, the windshield glass replacement was about $56.

There was no more playing baseball with a hardball for anyone on our street from then on. I cannot remember whose idea it was looking back there was even an adult watching the game....

Chapter 2

The Work Ethic – My Formative Years

My dad was for instilling a good work ethic in me, for which I am grateful. He was a mailman and then a piece butcher in the Vernon meat processing and packing district. My chores at home were the usual: make your bed, clean your room, wash the dishes, cut the lawn, etc. My first job at about seven years old was working in my father's friend's grocery market. It was within walking distance. His friend was a manager and lived on our street. I had the task of sweeping the floor. Once I swept the floor, I would find a spot to sit down. It had not been instilled in me the necessity to keep moving, stay busy as you are on the clock, earning your keep. I was let go after one day, having not understood the guidelines of my job, or when I should take a break etc. It was assumed I knew these things.

The next job my dad found for me, through another friend who lived in our block, was working in a dry cleaner. I was an errand boy. I would carry pressed clothes to the homes of customers nearby as a service, even deliver some pastries or a pie from the bakery located on the street of the dry cleaner.

I would get monetary tips for my work from those who received my deliveries. This all took place across town in Culver City. I also began learning how to press clothes after they were cleaned. This was during the summer when I was out of school. I do not remember why I did not return.

After moving to East 89th Street, my dad and mom met a few neighbors who knew how to play bid-whist a card game like spades. On occasion, those neighbors would come over and play Motown music, Jazz, dance, and play bid-whist. There was always drinking and alcohol available for those parties. I mentioned this because I took a special interest in watching the adults play bid-whist. I soon began to play bid-whist with the adults at around age 12. Our family moved to West 89th St. when I was at this age.

A year or so later, I had some junior high school friends who had paper routes, who helped me to get hired to earn some income. During this time, you had to have a bike, learn how to fold papers and machine string tie the newspapers, stack them and bag them. I found this to be a fun job as I learned.

The delivery route was sheer excitement, learning addresses, where to place the newspapers for each customer whether on the grass or on the porch. I had a knack for throwing newspapers and learning the system. We also made collections from the customer's monthly if they did not mail the amount in. I did well in this line of work.

However, a few admissions are in order. I did not have a bike, so my friends took care of that with me pairing up and riding along. The bike was not paid for, but rather lifted from someone's back yard. Also, after my friends finished their routes on Sunday mornings, fresh chocolate milk was left on some of the porches in the neighborhood by the delivery milk man. One of those would go missing. These things I am not proud of looking back…

On weekends from an early age, I participated progressively in groups such as the Woodcraft Rangers, Cub Scouts, and eventually the Boy Scouts. All of these were short-lived due to the availability of time and my interest. I really enjoyed playing football as a first sport, which really kept my interest.

I had some natural talent. My dad ran the quarter mile in high school and was a swimmer and springboard diver. In junior high I began playing basketball and evaluated my adaptation to a few things in gymnastics. When I became of age to take driver's education in school, it was exciting. I remember my dad used to put me on his lap when I was younger and let me steer the car when we were in remote areas. When it was time to get my driver's license, I passed the written and driving test the first time out. My sister received a car for her High School graduation. I remember getting the chance to drive her car when she was not using it.

When in high school, I stayed with football as a pickup sport but joined the c-level basketball team, moving up to varsity after a few years.

I was not exceptional in basketball, and did not see myself as going very far, so I left the varsity team.

I was just over 6 feet in height when graduating from high school. I grew 5 inches over the summer. It was a shock to me and my parents because I grew out of my pants. During the summer, I thought I would build up my wind/lung capacity, so on the weekends I would return to Washington High school where there was a coach, training runners in track and field events. I joined them to work on my sprinting, not knowing where the conditioning would lead me.

In the fall of 1968, I entered Los Angeles Harbor Junior College, in Wilmington, California. As I reflect, it is where my athletic career emerged. I had a high number in the draft lottery above 350 during the Vietnam War, so I wasn't called up to serve. As a result, I was able to enter college to further my education.

Many of my good friends I competed with in pickup basketball and in football games entered various branches of the service being selected with lower lottery numbers. These same friends went to parties, drinking beer or wine.

I remember having my first beer at around age 16. My parents knew I had begun drinking but did not seek to discourage me from going down that path, probably since it matched their lifestyle. My drinking was my choice, and it would develop into a problem years later. The family early on in my life went to church and me, my sister, and brother were taken as well. I had grandparents who were Christians.

My grandfather was a minister, but not in the role of a pastor or on staff serving a congregation. He was more of an evangelist - one who shares the good news of Jesus Christ. Around five or six years old my granddad sat me down very caringly and had me read a very important verse from the Bible and the gospel of John.

The word gospel means good news. The verse was John 3:3, which was spoken by Jesus to a religious leader of the Jews named Nicodemus. It said in part, "Most assuredly, I say to you unless one is born again, he cannot see the kingdom of God."

Since I was at a very young age, I only listened without asking a very important question of how does one become born again? There was no explanation given by my grandfather, but that verse would play a major role in my turning to God years later. During my first year in college, I didn't know what I wanted to be or what vocation I should pursue.

I remember taking classes in the machine shop, printing class, and electrical class in high school. So, I leaned toward Industrial Arts. I took classes along those lines and other classes to receive an eventual Associate of Arts degree. I had a physical education class which was required. I decided to take a physical ed elective to meet the requirements, which was basketball. I met some new people and a few associates from high school who came aboard, and our intramural team was formed. As an intramural team we, of course, competed against other teams.

All the competition occurred on the outdoor courts. Since I had trained over the summer after high school primarily running, I had good wind capacity and would run a quarter mile with ease. The basketball team I was on advanced to the intramural championship game. The college basketball coach was over the intramural basketball competition.

The team which I participated in won the intramural championship. The win was the first time I had won any organized competition. The coach invited each player on the team to come and try out for the varsity squad. About four of us accepted the invitation and ended up playing in a summer league at the college.

Three of the four made the team and entered the team practices. The other lost interest. Coach Jim White was once a player at USC and had a rigorous conditioning program.

He was a great teacher of basketball skills and as the preseason began, all the players were developing in the skills taught, and experienced incremental improvement. I became a starter and was placed at the center position, even though there was one other player returning from the previous season at 6'7".

I was close to 6'6" but had substantial leaping ability because of the rigorous training. Our team had a limited bench, so the starters played practically the whole game, unless we had a substantial lead. On a few occasions the starters set out for a breather through substitutions, during the game, playing two 20-minute halves.

Early in the preseason a few teams out mastered us as I remember, such as Compton College, Pasadena City College, and Cerritos College. The frontline of these colleges had a height advantage, experience, and more bench depth.

However, it challenged our team to grow and compete well in our league competition having encountered these teams in the preseason.
The greatest competition faced in our league was Los Angeles City College laced with talent in both their starters and a strong bench. The other team was Cypress College which had a 7-foot center by the name of Swen Nader. As the preseason ended, and the regular season commenced, our team began winning games. In our first game against Los Angeles City College, they handled us easily winning by 16 points. We played two games against Cypress, and our team won in close games. I remember fouling out in those games, but our guards Tony and Richard were unstoppable, and my backup player Howard did a fantastic job.

The last game of the season came down to playing Los Angeles City College for the league championship. Los Angeles City College had lost to Cypress College twice. We had to play City College on their home floor. If we win, Los Angeles Harbor College would be the sole first-place winner of our conference.

The night of that game, as we entered their house, I wondered what type of game I would have on their floor. Our whole team had improved and would leave everything we had on the court.

So, our team and theirs suited up. The gymnasium was packed when we came out for warm-ups. I remember seeing my sister and brother-in-law sitting in the stands. I had no idea they would be there.

The buzzer sounded and the game started. The game went back and forth. City College kept a small marginal lead throughout the game. Our team fought and fought but when the final seconds ticked off the game clock - LA City College had prevailed, winning by five points.

I had my best game of the season in the final game of the league competition. I scored 28 points and had 13 rebounds with some blocked shots. As a result of the loss there was a three-way tie for first place between Cypress College, LA City College, and LA Harbor College. The next challenge was entering the first game of the preliminaries to qualify for a shot at the Junior College State Championship. As a result of our loss to LA City College, our first game came against Compton College, which was undefeated. If LA City College lost to us, they would be playing Compton College.

Many Compton College players were at the final league game of ours, to see who they would be competing against in the state preliminary. LA City College, because of their win, would play San Diego Mesa College.

The day came for a rematch with Compton College. We were a better team after losing to them in a preseason game months earlier by 16 points. We really had our work cut out for us. Would we be able to even stay in the game and not be blown out? The front-line of Compton was 6'11", 6'9", and 6'5" and their guards were swift and could score. When the buzzer sounded, the gymnasium was packed. Compton was the dominant team early, but we were able to fight back. This game by far was the most exhausting game I had played to date. The defense needing to be played on their height, and my activity under the basket to score drained me.

We were able to get their 6'11" center in foul trouble, and our 6'7" forward was having a great game with all others contributing. The play clock showed 35 seconds left in the game with the score tied 74-74. It was time out, with the players all returning to the floor to finish the game. Unfortunately, I had nothing left in the tank. As I think back, had I been able to drink a fruit drink, a Gatorade, something to energize me and permit me to finish the game there may have been an upset. It was my role to go out to the half-court line once the ball was inbounded to one of our guards, he would pass to me coming up to the half-court line from our free-throw line. I didn't have the energy to go up and retrieve the ball. As a result, as our guard looked for me, the Compton guard stole the ball and went to his basket for a lay in. The same occurred as we inbounded the ball and a repeat of what had just occurred happened again. This time our guard fouling the Compton guard.

We did not advance the ball to position us to score in the final seconds. The clock expired and we lost the game by five points. This certainly was not the ending to a well scripted motion picture, with the cliff-hanging last shot to win the game. Compton College went on to win the state championship, having a record of 33 and 0 to end the 1970 season. Our forward ended up with 27 points, and I scored 13 points with 16 rebounds and a few blocked shots as our season ended. John Dearman, our 6'7" forward made 1st team all-conference and I made second team all-conference. I believe Tony Sanders was an honorable mention. Our record was 22 wins and 7 losses including the game lost against Compton College in the state preliminary.

Chapter 3

Some Awards in Athletics and Other Reflections

In the off-season a few of the track athletes asked me to come out for the team. It was indicated to me that, since I had long legs, I should be able to contribute to this area of sports. I thought I would humor them and started working out with them running in 40-yard sprints, long jumping, and practicing the triple jump. I realized I had no experience in the field events, but since I knew I had a good vertical leap that would carry over in the jumping events. The time came to start competing in the long jump and the triple jump. I believe my first meet jump was around 21 feet plus some inches. My first triple jump was around 44 feet plus, nothing to shout about. I kept working on the triple jump primarily, with the help of a trainer that came to the college in the afternoon and gave me some exercises to increase my extension. I want to follow instructions when one is trying to help me. The time came for the conference championship meet. I had been progressing in my jumps during the season. When my turn came up, I had my best jump to that point of 48'7" plus. I placed second in the competition and earned a trip to the state meet in Sacramento, California. I remember taking the same flight with the other qualifier from Harbor College who was a shot putter. During my event on my first jump, it was recorded at 49 feet 1 ¼ inches. The jump earned me a third-place position in the state meet that year in the triple jump. The winner of the triple jump was a friend of mine named James Butts, who I met as a Cub Scout years before.

The state meet ended the athletic competition for the season. I thought I would relax a bit for the summer, think about what I would do for work, and enjoy some boogie boarding at Redondo Beach. The summer before, my friend Howard, a basketball teammate, had some fun in this way. Just before classes would end at the college, I happened to see Coach White, and he asked if I was going to the athletic awards banquet that Friday. I told him I didn't think so. I wasn't much for events with a lot of people. I was more of a private person, so I was going to pass it up. He told me that I should come. I consented. Once I was there at the banquet, I found a seat with some of the athletes I knew.

We all were reflecting on what occurred during the basketball and track and field season.

Well into the presentation two awards remained. One was the Bob Kelly Memorial award for the athlete who accomplished the most for the college. I was stunned when my name was called. I had never received any type of individual athletic awards for anything I competed in. I delayed before going up to receive the award. After getting to the platform to receive the award, I was handed the microphone, and I was speechless. I told the audience I did not know what to say and handed the mic back to the presenter and exited the platform with haste. When seated I was relieved, but thankful for the award. The last award was the most valuable player at the college. The presenter began to give the reason for this award and for the second time I was asked to the platform to receive this award. You would think that I would be more poised, have more composure, have some words to say thanking my coaches in both sports, my teammates who assisted in the achievements of these awards, etc. All of this was unfamiliar to me. Unfortunately, here again, I was speechless and shocked having to stand in front of all those people. No one gave me a hint that any of what happened that evening would occur. I was unprepared, that this could happen to an ordinary guy like me.

I did not graduate from Harbor College at that time, even though I was there two years. Coach White wanted me to return for another season, which would give me two years active on the varsity basketball team. I told him I wanted to consider a four-year college having already been there two years. After my discussion with Coach White mail started coming in from four-year colleges offering scholarships in basketball primarily, but there were a few for track and field. I decided to go to Cal Poly State University at San Luis Obispo. It was out of the city approximately 200 miles up the coast. It had a beautiful and picturesque landscape of mountains, canyons, pastures, and nearby beaches. I was somewhat of an adventurer, wanting to explore a seemingly new world away from the big city of Los Angeles. Another reason, or I should say what focused my attention on this college, was it had a black track and field coach - Steve Simmons.

He was the only coach who made a point of visiting my home and arranged for me to fly up to the college at the request of the basketball coach. The 1960s was a time of black awareness, and a heightened sense to discover one's personal identity.

The saying of black is beautiful, the wearing of the natural hairstyle, Dashikis garments, and black power, resonated throughout the inner cities. Self-pride, education, and the need for unity and brotherhood were ideals. I can remember the time at Harbor College when a professor, Mr. Mann of African American studies, gathered many of the African American athletes and key students, and assembled us to go to the Dean of students' office because he declined to allow a black student union. The professor wanted to see if the Dean would decline the request to allow a black student union group at the college in front of all of those who came to his office. The Dean of students, with an intimidating show of support, reversed his decision.

I was 15 years old when the Watts riots broke out. My family had driven to Chicago to visit my uncle, aunt, and cousins. When we returned the tensions and emotions exploded in that area of the city. My grandfather still lived approximately 20 blocks south of 103rd St. and Hooper Street. My dad used to go night swimming at Will Rogers Park, right in that area. I can remember as a kid looking through the fence where my dad dived and swam. My sister and I were too young to participate in night swimming, so we would watch standing with our mom. The park was renamed Ted Watkins Memorial Park in 1995 after the founder of the Watts Labor Community Action Committee (WLCAC).[i]

I am one who never liked violence and does not advocate it. During the riots, 34 people were killed and more than 1,000 injured. The riot occurred August 11-16, 1965. Many stores were burned, and the business area ransacked. The city of Watts was named after the first railroad station built in the town. The Watts railroad station was built in 1904 on 10 acres of land donated by the Watts family. The town was incorporated in 1907.

The city voted to annex itself to Los Angeles in 1926. The city of Watts did not become predominantly black until the 1940s.[ii]

I settled into Stenner Glenn, a student housing unit off campus in San Luis Obispo.

I received a full ride athletic scholarship, and this was the best student housing offered. I was introduced around the complex and met others who were student tenants. I would have three seasons at Cal Poly. I switched my major to Industrial Technology, with a supervision concentration. In the nonconference games over the three years, I had the opportunity to go to places I never had been before. The first year the team flew to Utah and Colorado. The second year we went to Michigan, Illinois, and Virginia. The last year to Louisiana. The highlight in the games played during my time at Cal Poly during the preseason was against an All-American named George Gervin. He later was called the Iceman in the NBA. When our team visited Ypsilanti, Michigan to play Eastern Michigan University. It was during the winter, and it was 6°F outside. It was the coldest weather I had ever been in, up to that time, coming from a warm climate in Southern California. Mr. Gervin was electrifying. When the game ended, he put up 30 points and 20 rebounds. They beat our team by six points. We did not do so badly, yet we lost. I scored 20 points and 16 rebounds in that game. I remember one play on an open court where I was the last player between him and the basket. He went by me like I was standing still and laid the ball up on the square over the basket. I thought to myself – woe. After the game, some of his team members approached me and thought I had a decent game. Mr. Gervin never approached me, and I fully understand… He was the man.

My first year we went to the regionals and lost to University of Pacific. My best season was the following year. Three of our players Billy Jackson, Pinky Williams, and I, made First Team All-Conference and all District All America. We were an NCAA 2A small college. As I mentioned earlier in my story, I started drinking at the age of 16 years old.

All the other things introduced themselves progressively into my life; the girls, and the party life having entered college and sports notoriety. Every summer for about three years around my birthday I would have a birthday party for all the people I was meeting and some of those I met in sports. I never made it through my parties because I would always blackout. I no longer only drank beer and wine, but now in the off-season began drinking hard liquor such as mai-tais, black Russians, screwdrivers etc. My senior year was a total waste. One of our star player's Billy, was having a knee problem and was unable to play most of the season.

We did not have anyone to replace him. After our first season win, I had a party that same night. I had moved into an apartment with two other All-America athletes in track and field, Reynaldo Brown, a straddle high jumper with a best jump of 7'3", and Lowell Henry, a sprinter. Reynaldo also made the 1968 Olympic team. The following night we were to play Cal State Fullerton. It was not a wise decision to have a party after the Cal State Northridge victory. I should have gone to bed, but I was foolish and did not get the appropriate rest my body needed. The following night we lost to Cal State Fullerton by 24 points, our audience at home was silent and stunned. As the season continued things got worse, with more losses. There became infighting among me and a few of the players, and one of the fan's began to taunt me. Our fans and supporters diminished, and over the course of the season for home games the gymnasium would be empty. I thought I had a lot to do with the season going sideways by the wrong decision I made. I was a team leader and was to set the example for others. I could sense my motivation come game time decreasing. I did learn that when you are experiencing success, there are reasons for that success. Giving one's all, self-discipline, and making good decisions, which include and consider the other players and the fan base, are all part of it. I also recognized that some people look for your failure which can be caused by their own selfishness, or envy wanting what you have. When that is on the team it will be tough to succeed. My college basketball chapter was now closed. What would be next?

Chapter 4

Experience in Mexico

After the season in my final playing year in college, I played in a Pro League at Trade Tech College, over the summer. I pulled myself together and set my mind free of the frustrating season which had ended. After just a few games into the pro-summer league, I was approached by a few scouts from Guadalajara, Jalisco, Mexico offering an opportunity to play in the Mexican Professional Federation. The team they represented was Charros De Jalisco. I gave the offer some thought and made my decision to explore the opportunity in the country of Mexico. I was going through the application process with a company called AVCO at the time of the offer to play in the professional league in Mexico. Bobby Mac, a good friend of mine who played on the Harbor team, worked there, and recommended me. I still had a competitive spirit in me and thought about what a step up would bring as I reflected on the possibilities and challenge. I contacted the scouts, spoke about the pay, how it would come, and when was I expected to arrive. I was told I could be flown into Guadalajara, but I chose to drive my little Ford Cortina wagon. I was informed that another player named Alan Smith, had consented to play on the team. I had competed against him in my college league. Alan was 6'9", a leaper, dunk specialist, rebounder, and scorer. He would ride down with me. He played for Cal Poly State University at Pomona, our sister college.

When the day came for us to leave, it was the summer of 1973. I picked up Alan, we loaded up his things and departed. As we drove, we had our map, which took us through Calexico and from there into Mexico. We remember stopping at a motor lodge to cool off and take a shower, because we were driving through the Mexican desert. Our shower was with cold water, not knowing it to be the case when we checked in. As Americans we take a lot for granted having all the conveniences, to which we are so accustomed. As we traveled, we saw some of the people washing clothes at a riverbank and their homes were made from cardboard and scrap metal. I thought to myself that even our poorest can get food stamps, general relief etc. to help them pull through in tough times.

I wondered how did the people we passed by survive, and were they receiving any help from their government?

I remember driving on past the river area and back into the desert. It appeared to be in the 80°F - 90°F range and as we passed hills and very arid terrain, something happened to my car that brought us to a halt. The exhaust pipe had a crack in it near the generator and had fried it. So here we were, stuck in the Mexican desert hundreds of miles from home and stranded. Cell phones were not yet invented, there was no roadside emergency phone unit like in the states, so what could we do? We did not see very many cars on the two-lane road we were on. So, we waited. Before long, a vehicle stopped to assist us. We were offered a ride, driven to the next town and made a call to Prof. Duenas who was one of the scouts. I explained what had happened and he immediately decided for Al and me to receive tickets to fly into Guadalajara via Mexicana Airlines. Alan and I were kidding about the type of hissing beetle we came across as big as the beetles we have in the states flying around in the desert. Our imaginations were wondering what if we were stranded until nightfall. What would we encounter? We were glad it didn't come to that. We were basketball players, not specialists in survival and eating off the land.

As we approached the city at night, we could see the beauty of the city lights, a welcomed sight. We were picked up and shuttled away to our hotel accommodations. The following day our measurements were taken for our uniforms and warm-ups. We were driven to a practice facility and met the other players on the team. Another basketball player I competed against who played on the Compton College (33 and 0 State Championship) squad, was 6'11" Ron Richardson. He went on to Texas Tech on scholarship. He spoke about our prelim game to enter the state tournament. He told me that he thought they were going to lose that game. He said we were a very improved team than who they faced originally. But they prevailed as indicated.

The Mexican Professional Federation played under international rules, which made the hand a part of the ball. So, a foul on the hand in the U.S. would not be a foul by international standard. Three Americans could be on the court at any given time during play.

We had five players from the states on our squad and the best Mexican players from that city, who had competed in the league in earlier seasons with a few new additions. Our player-coach was an American named Adolphe, who could speak Spanish. We had a 12-member squad.

One notable currency comparison seen was the Mexican peso versus the U.S. dollar. Sixteen pesos was equivalent to one U.S. dollar. We were paid in U.S. dollars. We had spending money or per diem, plus the salary we earned. We ate well as athletes in Mexico. I enjoyed the Ranchero beefsteak platter, the filet mignon wrapped in bacon, porterhouse cut steak, the carne asada tacos, and the list continues. The price range for these dishes were $2-$4 U.S. A new home at the time could be purchased on the outskirts of the city having three bedrooms and two baths with a cobble stone driveway for $6,000 U.S. dollars. Many American retirees lived in Mexico during the time I was there. Lake Chapala was a retirement location near Guadalajara, which I had a chance to visit when sightseeing. I met some Americans living on retirement in Guadalajara.

The Mexican Professional Federation had a 64-game schedule for the 1973 season. There were professional teams in cities such as Agua Caliente, San Luis Potosi, Torreon, Districto or Mexico City, Leon, and Chihuahua. There may have been one or two other teams that I cannot recall. The team traveled by bus to each location. We had a few scrimmages with a Pan-American team visiting the area. While in Mexico, I played the small forward position, and if necessary, shooting guard. When the season started, we started with a 4 and 0 record. After a great start we lost some games. Ron Richardson became a player who scored over 40 points in a game, and he was included in the 40 points or more club. Alan Smith was noted for his offensive agility with his tip dunking and was an early mention for the All-Pro team. I became a consistent scorer and starter throughout the season. There were some American-seasoned players in Mexico we began to learn of, as we interacted playing against our opponents. Our team was not winning enough games to pack out the playing venue in Guadalajara. A problem arose when we were not being paid on time.

Halfway through the season Alan and Ron began to sit out and not play due to not being paid. The ownership promised to pay us, so I continued to play. Since Ron was married, and his wife being with him, after some time they decided to leave and head back to the United States. Alan decided to do the same after waiting didn't produce the results expected. They had traveled with the team to our opponent cities but when finding out the pay was not available; they were greatly discouraged.

Since the two of them sat out, I had to increase my scoring with the hope things would be made right. I am a person who will commit to something and trust that things will work out. I have a thing about holding up my end even to my own hurt. I stepped up my game, having games over 30 points, which were my highest points scored in any game in college or the pro league. My highest game was 36 points against Chihuahua, in Chihuahua. We had quite a scare in Chihuahua the second time around. We were leading in the game with the time expiring, and their star player hit a shot with no time on the clock which would tie the score. The officials at first said there was no time on the clock but then changed their mind. Our coaches did not want to hear any of it and had all the players grab their things and return to the bus. Once our team was inside the bus a few minutes passed and some of the fans began to throw rocks and bottles at our bus, cracking windows expressing their anger and hostility. The driver of the bus made haste, having started the engine earlier and we lit out of there to the road leading us back to our home city. Once on the road we all were expressing that we were glad to get out of there alive. Fortunately for us it was our last game in Chihuahua. We won some games and lost games with the addition of a few new players.

On days in between, I would be at the lady's bar, eating in restaurants, or surveying the city, with or without a guide. I met an American in the city that had been in Mexico for some time and had established a semi-precious stones business. He would buy Mexican opal, cats' eye, turquoise, agate etc. He would cut, polish, and sell the items. I took interest in what this American was doing. His name was David.

I took a trip with David to Monterey. I began to take some of the money I made and invested with David to learn his business. He began to train me on how to cut and polish stones with his lapidary equipment. He had a small laboratory in his living quarters. I did notice that David appeared to have an addiction to codeine. He would buy cough syrup from the pharmacy. He told me the reason for having to use it was to neutralize the source of pain he had. Sometimes he would appear catatonic.

As the season came near its end and concluded, I remember having to wait for payment. I remember being called to an office along with some other players to receive our pay.

The total amount owed was not given, rather a partial amount was given, and they wanted us to sign for the amount. I chose not to sign and was frustrated having given my all on the court. I walked out, never to see any of the representatives of the team again, knowing there was still money owed to me. I did not want to wait around for the final payment. I contacted David and prepared to pack up and depart from the city. David had given me a location in San Diego where he would meet me. I left my record player and albums with David that I had brought with me when I attempted to drive down to Guadalajara.

I departed the country of Mexico by train, with the intent to view the landscape of the country. The trip up to the states gave me an opportunity to reflect on another episode which was about to close in my life. My car remained in Mexico. There were positives to my experience in Mexico. I took note of the Mexican culture and friendliness, the closeness of family life, the traditional Sunday stroll in the various squares of the city, the architecture and cathedrals, The Mariachis, the shopping district, the carne-asada tacos fried by street vendors using their self-contained mobile carts, the housing district and tourist areas. These things showed me the positive side of the Mexico experience overall.

There is one other side I am too embarrassed to speak about. (Review Location Map #1 after Reference Credits). I thought about what life would be like back in the states.

Where would the association with David lead, and what would the future hold? All these thoughts were a mystery, as one would turn another page into a nonfictional story wondering what would be next. I had complete uncertainty but not for long…

Chapter 5

Meeting Some Celebrities

I can remember vaguely reentering the United States through Tijuana and making my way back to Los Angeles. Upon returning I stayed with my father and stepmom, in the house where I had lived since the age of 12. I was faced with three opportunities which I could pursue. I first would follow up on the business I was learning from David, with the semi-precious stones. I did meet him in San Diego as we had planned, but I was not ready for what occurred when we did meet. David's condition had deteriorated, he appeared doped up and paranoid. In our meeting very little was said. He transferred to me about ¼ of a jar of uncut and unpolished Mexican opals, which I received. I knew in my heart that the opportunity which appeared promising was beginning to fade. I was never brought in to meet any of those David had as a customer base. He had received the funds I gave him, had given me some training as to how to cut, power sand, and polish the various stones but that was as far as he had taken me. I had been taken to one location for the purchase of opals, which was in Monterey, but no place further. It became apparent that David was not really seeking a partner in his business. The meeting with David was the last time I would see him. The hope that I once held diminished almost as fast as it appeared to materialize.

Even though, this so-called opportunity suddenly ended, I thought to myself how many people from south-central Los Angeles had learned anything about semi-precious gems with the firsthand experience of cutting, sanding, and polishing to the product grade of marketing them. There was no mention of this type of class in the high school I attended. I am sure David's lapidary equipment was rudimentary, but the experience furthered my personal knowledge in an area never explored by me.

The second area of opportunity once returning to the Los Angeles area was a call by my former basketball coach from Cal Poly. He must have known I had returned from playing in the Mexican Professional Federation, or it was sheer coincidence.

It was communicated to me that a team in Spain wanted to sign an American player to play in the continental league in Europe or a professional team to travel within Spain. I wasn't sure which was the case. I thought here is another adventure to a location I have never been.

During the time I was being offered the opportunity to play in Europe, my old roommate from college had assembled a team and had been touring with Motown artists playing celebrity basketball for charitable purposes. One of the player's was also a former roommate of mine. The three of us were the same friends mentioned earlier, who were All Americans in track and field, named Lowell and Reynaldo. Lowell was starting a charitable venture for the mentally challenged youth. Lowell had the persuasive gift of gab. He was fearless in approaching people that had achieved stardom. I can remember while at Cal Poly he arranged for the Temptations to do a charitable concert through Berry Gordy Jr., the founder and chairman of Motown record company at the time. I had reserved the wine cellar for an after party at the famous Madonna Inn. I still remember the artistic rock structures in various suites with waterfalls. While at Cal Poly one of the students gave a party in one of the suites. It was impressive and quite spacious. The Inn had its own class A restaurant and a bakery which could rival any I've ever experienced. The Temptations did not attend the after party. As I remember, they needed to return to Los Angeles after their performance. Word of mouth spread regarding the after party at the Madonna Inn and once the concert ended the wine cellar was packed with partygoers. My memories of the close associations I had with my former roommates, the charitable worthy cause, an opportunity to meet and play with celebrities, persuaded me to stay in Los Angeles and join Lowell and Reynaldo. I did not have a clue as to where all this would lead, but I was willing to find out.

Some of the players on the team consisted of Jackie and Tito Jackson, their cousin Pewee, Berry Gordy IV, Diana Ross's brother Chico, and some sitcom stars. Marvin Gay was the coach. Michael sat in the stands. As the celebrity team played at various venues, I was given the opportunity to accompany Lowell and Reynaldo to homes of various Motown recording artists such as Diana Ross, the Jackson Five, and Marvin Gaye.

I also found out that Lowell had been assisting the son of Berry Gordy in his sprint technique. This led to an invitation to Mr. Gordy's home for an introduction. Lowell wanted me to come after all the formalities had been done, so I did. I eventually was introduced to Mr. Gordy Jr. Lowell, Reynaldo, and I had an open invitation to come to the Gordy home through Berry Gordy IV.

Alongside the Gordy home was a long stretch of grass which very slightly had a gradual incline. The area was a perfect place to practice sprinting. Berry IV, Lowell, Chico, and I would sprint about 40 yards on that stretch of grass, racing. When we went to the Gordy's home, we would run and shoot around with the basketball in the driveway that widened as it reached the car garage. What none of us were aware of was Mr. Gordy was observing the activities upstairs, overlooking the 40-yard grass area on the side of the home and the area overlooking the driveway where we would shoot around. Mr. Gordy had told Lowell that he had participated in some boxing growing up. To be a boxer, one must be quite competitive and tough. Lowell, Berry IV, Chico, and I got a chance to see Mr. Gordy's competitiveness firsthand. Mr. Gordy wanted to race Berry IV and Chico in a sprint on that 40-yard stretch of grass. Neither I, nor anyone else, had any idea of what we were about to see. When the words were expressed - get on your mark, get ready, set, go! Mr. Gordy in the first 10 yards was out running Chico and was not too far behind Berry, his son. We were simply amazed that Mr. Gordy came out in a robe like one as if he were getting ready to box an opponent. In this race he almost scored an upset. Mr. Gordy stayed close to his son of 18 years and Chico was of similar age almost the entire race. After this event occurred, Mr. Gordy asked Lowell and I if we knew much about beach volleyball. At the time we knew only that beach volleyball was a popular sport. Another door was opening unexpectedly.

Mr. Gordy inquiring about beach volleyball and wondered if professional volleyball could sustain itself. It was an unanswerable question. Yet Lowell and I seized upon the opportunity to explore, through research, its possibility. During the 1970s there was no Internet, as we have today.

In pursuing research about beach volleyball, it had to be done at the library. Lowell's strength was the gift of gab opening the door of opportunity. My gift, so I began to learn, was taking research, organizing it, and putting it on paper. Upon gathering all the data available a report was developed. While on the way to a volleyball match in Santa Monica, following Mr. Gordy, Lowell jumped out of our car to give Mr. Gordy the report.

Mr. Gordy liked what he read and decided to pursue attending more volleyball matches. Mr. Gordy wanted Lowell and I to come as well. In a matter of weeks Lowell and I were given an assignment to search out a coach for his pro volleyball team and a general manager.

Interviews were scheduled to meet with Mr. Gordy at his Motown Hollywood offices. After different individuals were interviewed, he decided on a player-coach named Rudy Suwara, and a general manager by the name of Sandy Geis. With the hiring of these two individuals Lowell and I completed what was asked for and were compensated for our work.

During this time, and it was quite a coincidence, my mother, a licensed vocational nurse, was doing private duty at the Gordy home taking care of Mr. Gordy's father who was referred to as Pops. Whenever we would come across his path in the home, he would refer to us as the boys. We would have short spurts of interaction with him whenever the occasion presented itself. Pops would always tell us to put good gasoline into our cars because bad gasoline would reduce the life of the car. While involved with Mr. Gordy and the charitable endeavor to assist the less fortunate, my life was in a state of flux. Lowell and I were attempting to establish the All-American foundation, but I had to move from my dad's home to my mom's home, who both had remarried. Since Lowell was still involved in sprinting, he had organized the All-American track club. I worked out in preparing for running with the club in all-comers meets. We had a 4x100 relay team. I ran as one of the 100-yard legs. I remember running in my sweatpants during a work-out at the UCLA football, track and field stadium and was timed 9.8 seconds in the 100-yard dash. I was surprised, having never been clocked at this distance. I got my speed from my dad. I remember working out with Willie Decker one evening, and he told me I should have been a sprinter.

Willie was a world-class star sprinter at USC. I remember him clocking 9.2 seconds in the 100-yard dash, and 20.2 in the 220-yard dash in a meet against their cross-town rival UCLA.

Sometime later, I did not have a dependable source of income. I was still involved in the nightlife, and those things associated with it. I began to feel an emptiness inside, and felt I was missing something, but could not put my finger on it. The life I was living was not satisfying.

I was under the impression that alcohol, girls, and partying would satisfy my inner longing. Finding work was usually not a problem for me. It so happened that after a few weeks at my mother's home, the Carson mall opened, and I applied at JC Penney and was hired to work in the sporting-goods department. The position at the Penny company brought some stability financially, but I still knew there was something missing. Lowell and I were still working on sponsorship for the All-American foundation. We approached Muhammed Ali first by letter, then an opportunity came to attend his victory party in 1975. The fight he won was dubbed the "Thrilla in Manilla" against Joe Frazier.

Lowell also had met Nancy Wilson, the famous jazz singer, and we developed a plan for the foundation which she had a chance to review. Before meeting Mr. Ali, what I was looking for to fulfill that emptiness found me. It was not sought by me, and if one were to ask me what I was missing at that time in my life, I would not have given what I found as my answer....

Chapter 6

Finding What was Missing

I had come home from some late-night experience, laid on the couch not going upstairs to bed. When I awoke, everything was quiet in the house. It was a Sunday morning, sometime around 9 AM. I flipped on the television and the station was on channel 9. A TV minister was speaking about future events from the Bible. He caught my attention because he was behind a desk, sharing about an event coming to Earth called the tribulation. His name was Doug Clark. I was already aware of the two places one could end up once they physically died, but I knew very little if anything about a coming day on Earth called God's wrath for the accumulation of mankind's rebellion and sinfulness. I knew I was guilty of sins I committed. I had to be real. He spoke about catastrophic upheaval on the Earth as had never occurred. The devastation of war anyone would understand and that was going to occur from the speaker during this time, but when there are asteroids in quantity striking Earth, and earthquakes occurring at magnitudes to move every mountain and island from its fixed location, you have my attention.

During this period, the judgments of God will progressively worsen. The Earth's vegetation would become scarce, portions of the oceans would be polluted, and sea life would die. Ships in the sea would be destroyed, freshwater sources would also become polluted, diseases would occur. Earth's population would be substantially reduced. All that would occur was to bring about a repentant heart in humanity. God would save those who would respond to the message of repentance and acceptance of His Son who died for humanity on the cross. When hearing about the things, which were said by Doug Clark, I did not want to experience anything that would occur in that period. He said one could escape that horrific period. What really triggered my response was when he gave the good news of Jesus Christ and the fact that one needed to be born again to enter the Kingdom of God and become a spiritual/relational child of God.

As I was seated on the couch, my memory caused me to return to the day my grandfather had sat me down and read to me the passage in John 3:3, about the necessity of being born again to enter the Kingdom of God.

At the end of the message delivered by Minister Clark, he asked the TV audience if they wanted to enter a spiritual relationship with God through Jesus Christ? If so, we could follow him in a prayer of repentance, asking for forgiveness and inviting Jesus Christ into one's heart. I realized at that moment I needed to pray and invite Jesus into my life. Just before Minister Clark recited what those in the audience would follow, I dropped to my knees and followed in prayer speaking aloud as he spoke the words that changed my life and eternal destiny. My custom was to head to the refrigerator to get a can of beer and prepare for sports viewing. It was the spring of 1975. Typically, at this time I was waiting for a pro basketball game, having played the sport. When I pulled the can from the refrigerator a soft voice in my mind said, "Robert, you don't need this anymore." The voice stopped me, having caught me off guard. I thought for a moment and decided to obey the voice. I was very close to becoming an alcoholic. A beer at 9:30 AM, what do you think? From that time on I never had another beer. I can remember having a small glass of champagne to toast an associate's wedding celebration, whose name was John Smith, a world-class quarter miler and record holder at the time, but no alcohol after that. I still had some issues with women being a single man and in a relationship at that time, but in time that area was brought under control. I had to break off the relationship I was in. Because I wanted to stop having physical relations, she ended up leaving me. After receiving Christ, I really did not know what to do. It was put in my mind to start reading the Bible. I did not attach to any church at the time because I was unfamiliar with where to start going. As time progressed, I met a very attractive woman at JC Penny's, who worked upstairs in children's clothing. Pam would become my wife in time. She had come to Christ in December of the same year as I. She was from a respected middle-class family, great parents, an older brother, and younger sister. After God worked on cleaning up my life, Pam became the only woman that I would love and remain faithful to. As one seeks to follow the Lord God, God works on his or her behalf.

As time continued, I moved out to an area close to my future wife, participated in group Bible study, met some of her Christian friends, and stayed fixed on learning the Bible. My calling to the ministry wasn't without resistance. While still at my mother's and stepdad's, I began getting little indicators from a person I worked with who was a Christian.

He told me that God had a plan for my life and there was a Christian who had a prophetic ministry coming to his church. He invited me to come, so I went.

I was called up to the podium the second night along with the person that had accompanied me. The minister shared some things with me that indicated God had a work for me. Other things were said, but I thought about it and felt I would not be a person God would call, because I was a quiet person, shy, not very vocal, not very smart. I continued to offer excuses of "not me." Early one morning around 2 AM or so, God is my witness, I was awakened by a surge of heat moving from my feet up through my body to the crown of my head. It was so hot, not because of the night air, which was cool in my room, but because this was not natural, but something supernatural. I had to immediately come out from underneath the covers of my bed. As I stepped out of the bed all I could hear sounding off within my head was, "You are going to preach the gospel." "You are going to preach the gospel." I broke down and knew I had been called to preach the gospel of Jesus Christ. With all my past baggage, shortcomings, sinfulness, and inadequacies, God had selected one who was unworthy of such a calling. If I were to lay aside what I knew to be true, I would be fighting against the will of God. I didn't know the first thing about being a minister of the gospel, but in time I would learn. I remember while at the home of one of Pam's friends named Verna, who also became a friend of mine, a Bible study was being held.

One day, while we were gathered, a knock on her door was heard. At the door was this short man named Dewey, who we came to know after our introduction. It was the first time any of those participating in the study had met Dewey.

He was invited into Verna's home, and he shared what he was doing. He was in the neighborhood sharing the gospel or good news about Jesus. My interest was piqued. Dewey informed me that there was an inner-city ministry named United Gospel Outreach in Los Angeles. The director was Joe Curtis, who also owned the Christian bookstore with his wife in the same location. I was invited to meet minister Curtis and participate in the outreach occurring in south-central Los Angeles. I accepted the invitation. A few months before Dewey came across us, I had been seeking God's leading through prayer and fasting.

I continued to read and study God's word. In the meantime, I continued meeting for Bible study at Mrs. Hale's home with our small group. We visited various churches where the Spirit of God was at work. One church minister was well-known where we attended.

It was in that church facility, during an evening service, I was anointed by the Spirit of God to witness in a powerful way.

I remember going to an evening service in one church where the minister was teaching the word of God, and while everyone was seated, a demonically possessed man entered the right aisle of the church, and everything stopped. The minister teaching stared at the possessed man and the possessed man stared at him. Everyone seated was looking back and forth to see what was about to occur. I neither saw anything like what I was about to see, nor have I seen anything like it since. The minister stood in the front and moved from behind the podium and came in front of it. The demonically possessed man walked down the aisle and upon reaching the minister, the minister said, "In the name of Jesus." After those words, God is my witness, and everyone else who was present, saw with their own eyes the demon-possessed person lifted off the ground into the air, being supernaturally suspended about five feet horizontally. After which, he was quickly flung to the ground with the minister jumping upon the man to cast out the demonic spirit. The minister was assisted by some of the deacons as the battle went on for the release and possession of the man. I thought that the minister would prevail by the name of Jesus. But I learned, as was in this case, some demons will not come out except by fasting and prayer.

Looking back, I thought maybe the minister was not prayed up and had not been fasting. Or maybe the possessed man was not willing to be released. God knows. Demons are only subject to the name of Jesus,[2] but one needs to know Jesus first, and to be ready when they are encountered by the demonic. The same demon-possessed man came to the church of a well-known pastor. As the pastor was giving his message, I noticed that something caught the attention of the pastor. I, and a few others with me, sat on the balcony. When I looked around a few rows back, the same demon-possessed man I had seen at the other church had stood up, which distracted the pastor.

When I saw how this was a hindrance to the pastor, I looked at the demon possessed man and told him to sit down in the name of Jesus, and he sat down.

I know these events must sound like something taken from a movie, but I assure you these things occurred, just as I am a real flesh and blood human being writing my story. There is no need for me to lie about these matters, because I will have to stand before Christ and give an account of the things done in my body, both good and bad as a believer. During this time, a pleasant occurrence happened in my life, when my brother needed a place to stay having some problems at my mom's. He lived with me for a brief time, and very soon while living with me, I had the privilege of leading him to Christ. Afterward my brother received a call to the ministry, and in time started reaching out to the poor and downcast. He organized ministry in the park to reach the unchurched, had clothing give a-ways, fed the homeless on what is called skid-row in downtown Los Angeles, enlisting the help of Sub-Way sandwich franchise and In-N-Out Burger. He, along with others assisting, shared the good news of peace with God through Jesus Christ. I had a chance to participate in the outreach my brother conducted.

---

[2] Acts 19:11-20

Chapter 7

Early Ministry Experiences

On several occasions I met Dewey to knock on doors of those in various neighborhoods out where I lived. I would also drive down to the United Gospel Outreach (U-GO) in Los Angeles. I and others would pair up and speak to those on the street and in their homes about the need to come to Christ out of His love for us, having laid down His life, so we can be forgiven and escape eternal punishment for our sins. This is the greatest and purest love story of all time. His sacrificial love never fails in saving even the lowest sinner and will be remembered throughout eternity.

There was one person I remember coming to Christ named Raymond. His conversion was extraordinary, not at all what occurs with new converts, in general. When Raymond accepted Christ, his eyes were brightened as if light were shining out of him. As he began to attend Bible study it was obvious God was doing a special work in this new believer. His eyes glistened. The ways of God are so multifaceted we never can know why He works a certain way with some who He brings to Himself, and differently with others. God's ways are above our ways and His thoughts above our thoughts.[3] I began spending increasing time at United Gospel Outreach to the extent that Joe Curtis allowed me to live over the bookstore. I had left JC Penney's, and with my call and new direction, I had put the sinful lifestyle behind me. My calling began to conflict timewise with the direction of the project Lowell had and was pursuing while I was still at my mom's. I sensed I needed to let that go. So, I did. While at United Gospel Outreach, where I spent a little less than a year, I participated in outreach ministry with one of the bookstore worker's whose name was Samuel. Sam gave me good Bible study tools to better understand the word of God. We also had a film ministry going to churches and parks to show evangelistic or good news films. After the film, Samuel would share the necessity of our needing to receive Jesus Christ for forgiveness of one's sins, and acceptance into the spiritual family of God.

---

[3] Isaiah 55:8-9

We went door-to-door, passing out Christian tracts and speaking in neighborhoods.

I remember sharing my testimony at Union Rescue Mission in downtown Los Angeles and holding a luncheon for the ministers to raise funds for a drug treatment facility in south-central.

During the summer, a government-sponsored youth program was applied for and granted. We interviewed teenagers and accepted fifteen teen youths, both girls and boys. We were able to go on field trips, a summer camp at Quaker Meadows in the nearby mountains, and share with the youth the word of God. The young people were paid and had some chores of cleaning the facility, helping with mailing lists, etc. As the year continued, I found a part-time job at a Mennonite Christian School on Manchester Boulevard. I was a custodian. It was a very humiliating experience, but it was a test. It lasted for about four months. After that I was hired as a youth counselor at a youth home, whose capacity was 48 young men. During this time, I began taking courses at a Bible Institute - Grace Bible Institute, in Long Beach. I also took two classes at Biola College.

There were two unique experiences I had while living at United Gospel Outreach. When I came to the Union Rescue Mission, I met one of the mission's counselors. His name was Ron. Sam, and I would pray occasionally in one of the rooms in the U-GO ministry building. Ron joined our prayer group and the three of us became friends. We all engaged in intense prayer that God would move in the community to bring people to Christ for salvation. We were praying primarily on weekdays. Monday to Friday, we also fasted. We all were praying that God would disrupt the forces of darkness and tear down the deceptions placed in the minds of those who had not believed. One night, while I was sleeping, my air was cut off and I could not breathe. Since I was still asleep, I began to suffocate. I sensed there was a presence upon me, so in my mind I began to say, "I rebuke you in the name of Jesus." "I rebuke you in the name of Jesus," until it came out of my mouth, at which time the presence lifted off me, and I could breathe. No one else was in the building. It was dark, so I turned on the light, and saw nothing. I was sleepy, so I laid back down after turning off the lights.

I thought it was over...

Once I was back to sleep the same thing happened to me again with the same results.

Understanding that an invisible demonic spirit was attacking me, I realized I had to expel the entity from the building for it to never return in the name of Jesus. So, I walked through the whole building pleading the blood of Jesus and reciting that the demonic force could not remain on the premises, commanding it to leave never to return. I went back to sleep and never had that experience again. The Scripture says that Christians overcome by the blood of the Lamb, which is figurative for Jesus, and by the word of our testimony.[4] We also, are to submit to God. Resist the devil and he will flee from you. (James 4:7.) We are to resist steadfast in the faith.[5] If you are not a born-again Christian, do not attempt to confront demonic forces. Review what happened with the 7 Sons of Sceva in Acts 19:11-16. Our prayers were seeking good but had attracted evil.

I am an ordinary believer in Christ, no one special from my own eyes, who loves the Lord. I have no power alone over satanic entities other than in the power which comes through Christ and His name – (Luke 10:17-20). God, however, values His people and all humanity, because we are made in His image, even though we are fallen. His spiritual family are those who have come to Christ. God uses instances like the one earlier outlined, to train those he wants to use and to strengthen our faith.

I know some are thinking that I am making up the experiences being shared. Or do you think I have lost my mind? There is no time for games, your soul is your most valuable possession. What does it profit a man or woman to gain the entire world, but in the end lose their soul?

---

[4]Ref. Revelation 12:11
[5]Ref. 1 Peter 5:8-9

There is an invisible realm where God desires your good to be with Him now and in eternity, and Satan your demise to remain with him and spend eternity with him in torment. God has already won, and Satan has lost. Read Revelation chapter 20. What one does with Christ in this life determines where one spends the next life. Jesus says, "He who is not with me is against Me, and he who does not gather with Me scatters abroad." (Matthew 12:30). There is no neutral ground.

Here is another incident, unrelated to what was shared earlier, while living at United Gospel Outreach.

I was asleep again, and I heard a loud screeching of tires, and two vehicles collide. The next thing I know is one of the picture windows in the building broke either by a person running through it, or a brick being hurled into it. I heard shouting and voices saying, "get him!" As I got downstairs fumbling and still half asleep, someone was in the main office and there was a door between me and him. When he tried to come through the door, I held it shut, not knowing if the person had a weapon, and if those after him would end up including me. So, I held onto the doorknob, but the man was bleeding and convinced me he needed help. I then released the door, and he came through and went out the back door of the facility, while those who seem to want to pursue the man were stopped by what I shouted. I said, "I'm calling the police!" As you can imagine that ended any attempt to come through the broken window area. In the morning there was this large broken picture window, it must have been 6' x 8'. I hate to think what would have happened to the injured man if the other men had gotten to him. There were no vehicles out front at day light that were in the collision. There was evidence of a crash with broken glass in the street from what collided. When Joe arrived, he was glad no more damage had occurred, and that I was safe. The picture window was replaced, and the ministry continued. I was licensed at United Gospel Outreach to preach the gospel of Jesus Christ and felt my calling at that time was in evangelizing or sharing the good news of peace with God through Jesus Christ.

Chapter 8

Biblical Training, Marriage, and Work

At the end of 1979, I needed to find my own apartment. I was attending the Bible Institute and moved to live in the vicinity of the Institute. I moved to Long Beach. I also found another place of employment to keep some income flowing. My major was Christian education. It was not long before the opportunity came to work in construction at an oil refinery by the name of Champlin. The job also paved the way for Pam and me to marry, which occurred in the summer of 1981. I continued pursuing my Christian education major at the Institute and worked. My wife took some classes and worked. We were doing fine as a couple, but I started wanting a vehicle that would provide income, so I could be self-supported in the ministry to spread the gospel. I remember Paul was a tent maker and had supported his missionary team by his trade/vocation. As the job at Champlin oil refinery was completing its expansion project, I had to find another area to work. I went into route sales with a bottled water company named Bastanchury Waters. I spent nine years with this company. The first day hired, the manager road with me, showed me how to keep records, it was an easy fit for me as shoes on my feet. The route had just lost a 700 bottle per month stop, which left the route with only 500 bottles per month, making it the smallest route in the Long Beach branch. My areas for delivery to work were Compton, Watts, Willow brook, Southgate, Cudahy, and a few other areas of south L.A. My granddad, now in heaven, had lived on 123rd St, a few streets south of Martin Luther King Hospital. My wife Pam and I lived in his home, left to my dad and uncle. Monthly rent was paid, and we settled in at that location for the next five years.

A 500-bottle route did not produce very much income, so I set out to change that with God's help. I was given an approach to growing the route, which was the star approach. I was to speak to every customer's neighbor, which is the three across the street, and the two homes next door. When in a business or commercial area, I progressively sought to talk to every prospective decision-maker.

I made them an offer after letting them sample our product, and many consented to the extent my route doubled and then tripled all in the same year. My product was less expensive and of equal quality to my competitors. The work was rewarding, and I attribute this to my father having ingrained in me a good work ethic. My dad used to share with me that dirty hands (i.e., working with my hands) is a mark of an honest man. I know this sounds like an oxymoron. At the end of the first year, my route customer books were audited.

I had a few of the other sales associates kid me that I must had been setting up phone booths as customers. I did not know why a comment like that was made. So, I just smiled. I wasn't aware that some who had routes cheated on their books. One was fired.

I was not aware that at the end of every year a corporate dinner was held near the headquarters in Fullerton. It was always just before Christmas, typically at a country club. On that night, my wife and I dressed for the occasion and attended the soirée. There was music and dancing, drinks, and a delicious dinner. Of course, I did not drink any alcohol. After those events, the awards portion of the evening came. The company employed 74 route drivers at the time, which extended into the San Fernando Valley, all of Los Angeles, Inland Empire, Orange County, and Blythe. The management awards were given out, then the route salesman branch awards were given out. The last award to be given was the route salesman of the year award. Since I was not called as the route salesman for my branch, I sensed that I may receive the overall route salesman of the year award. My thoughts didn't betray me. I was selected as the top overall route salesman of the year. When called up to receive the award, I was able to express a few words of thanks to my Lord Jesus Christ for helping me to accomplish the award. It was short and not like what had occurred earlier in my life. The following year I received the branch route salesman award. In due course I developed a marketing plan, which I thought could cause exceptional customer growth for the company. It was a network marketing approach. I had dabbled in network marketing, thinking that it could develop into a lucrative business to support me full-time in ministry, giving me greater flexibility.

I approached the president of the company, Charles Soderstrom. The concept intrigued him, but I did not have all the answers to ensure its success. The concept was not implemented. What happened was a promotion for me.

A substantial number of the accounts I established were commercial accounts. I was taken off my route and made a commercial accounts specialist. I did well, and received another promotion to train a few other salesmen, supervise them, and expand the commercial accounts base for the company and households using our product. I was moved to the corporate office as my base of operations.

My wife and I moved to Lakewood which was closer to the corporate, and our in-laws assisted in helping us purchase a condo with a down payment. As time preceded, I didn't complete my BA in Christian education. I was 15 units short. My dabbling in network marketing was a distraction. My wife and I continued serving at Christian Fellowship of Los Angeles, where I was ordained as a minister of the gospel of Jesus Christ. I worked with the youth and helped in spreading the gospel in the neighborhoods around the church. On occasion I was able to deliver a sermon to the congregation. I was busy with work and ministry still looking for a way to expand the message of the gospel and to eventually reach the world.

In 1989, my wife and I began looking for a home in the Riverside County area. My in-laws had moved out to that area. Earlier that year we had our first child, so we wanted to own our own home. The water company had a branch in Colton, so I transferred and worked out of that branch which served the eastern portion of the Inland Empire down to Temecula. My wife and I talked over the opportunity, and the move was made. The same model I worked under in Fullerton, I carried to the Colton branch with the consent of my superior, the sales manager, and VP Jeff Spittel. Jeff came to one of our church services in the Los Angeles area to observe and satisfy his curiosity regarding the Christian faith. Jeff was a very personal and skilled sales professional and had invited my wife and I to his home, being married himself.

He was a former college football player and had a try-out with the pros. I can remember when the president was considering a name change for the company, some names were floating around. Eventually, the name became Yosemite Waters. Jeff would say people would not be able to pronounce the name. Jeff was from the eastern portion of the U.S., not a native Californian.

He thought people would pronounce the new name as Yo-So-Mite. Not Yosemite. It was humorous. Some years passed, and things were a bit above average. It was different from Fullerton, due to the Orange County area having higher income per capita than the area overall now being worked. I remember Jeff coming out to the Colton branch and pulling me aside. He said he would be leaving the company, something regarding a disagreement with the president. Jeff moved back to the eastern portion of the country. He, being married and familiar with the area, thought it would be a good place to settle. One year or so passed and I received a call from Jeff, and he is back in Southern California. He and his wife decided the East Coast was not for them.

Jeff became the sales manager for a company named Presentation Products, located in Santa Fe Springs. I was intrigued with what he presented to me, spoke about it with my wife, and decided to leave the company I had been with for almost a decade. I love new opportunities that could expand my skills and knowledge base, with a challenge. Presentation Products was a visual aids company targeting businesses, military, warehouses and schools with electronic equipment and systems for giving presentations and presentation support. The products that were being marketed were LCD panels and projectors, poster printers, lettering and labeling systems, lecterns, manual and electronic easels, PA, and speaker systems, with assorted other support products. My bread-and-butter was the poster printers and the lettering/labeling system combo, which schools could use in classrooms as a teaching aid, for announcements, and advertisements. Teachers could use posters with an easel for bullet point presentations of a lesson. The ASB (Associated Student Body) and other departments would use the system for their interests and needs of event promotions and advertisement.

The company which manufactured the poster printer and labeling system was named Varitronics. Every year Varitronics would reward the nation's top producers with an all-expenses paid trip to some exotic location. Typically, the trips would be a cruise in the Caribbean or flight to an island in the Pacific and last for 7 to 8 days. I became a sales consultant in mid-1991. By the end of 1992, I had won my first trip beyond the boundaries of the Continental United States, to the U.S. Virgin Islands of St. Thomas and St. John. It was a 7 - day cruise. The trip was a first for me leaving the Continental United States, other than Mexico. My wife and daughter accompanied me on the cruise. The cruise will come at a time when the hurricane season had ended, so the trips were in March or April, if in the Caribbean. The time came when we left on a flight to board our cruise ship in Florida. It was with Norwegian Cruise lines. We boarded with the others from around the country who were representatives of the top producers in the nation. I met one of the ones in my region who was a competitor. He was a rep from Minnesota Western. We were cordial to one another, but we did not become buddies. Both of us had respect for each other and both of us submitted bids on some of the same schools and military installations. I can remember taking my father-in-law with me to Fort Irwin outside of Barstow to do a presentation, him being a former military service man. It was a nice trip for the two of us, since I usually traveled alone to areas all over Southern California. I had a great transportation vehicle which was gas efficient, a 1992 Honda Accord LX. The cruise was an enjoyable experience. I learned some things about the Caribbean. The first is that a storm can come upon a cruise ship in a manner of minutes and end within a 10-minute period. This occurred on our cruise. Another thing that was fascinating was the clear blue water and the visible sea life when snorkeling. The pictures in magazines are not exaggerated. The beauty is breathtaking. While surveying the island of St. Thomas, we made our way by vehicle to an observation location high in elevation overlooking a cove with a sandy beach area. While at the observation site, we saw a stretch of other islands laid out across the Caribbean. It was amazing. As we descended the location, we were able to overlook the bay where our ship had docked and noticed there were other cruise ships at port and some yachts going out and coming in.

The air was crystal clean and fresh, with the rich influence of the ocean's scent.

The following day many from our group boarded the shuttle craft with the capacity of about 50 people, to survey the Isle of St. John. The water was a rich marine blue and pristine. We toured the island and one of the most visited sites was the remnant of the slave quarters. St. John is the smallest of the U.S. Virgin Islands. There was not much to see on the island. The island has a small population of black slave ancestry from the slave trade which occurred centuries earlier.

We went to a few of the shops on the island and then headed back to St. Thomas to board our cruise ship. (Review Location Map #2 after Reference Credits).

We were soon on our way back to the States. When we reached the port, we entered the US customs station after we disembarked. I showed my identification and began to speak up for my wife and daughter. The customs agent asked me to let them speak up for themselves. He wanted my wife to answer him directly and state whether they were returning from a nice cruise. After considering the method the agent employed, I realized the way to detect whether one is possibly not a citizen of the U.S. is to let them speak. The customs agent is skilled in detecting the accent of a non-resident, even though some U.S. residents may have an accent. In that case he would then ask for the credentials of the person and do his due diligence. For us the agent let us pass reasoning we were who we said we were.

The following year my family and I would be on our second cruise with Varitronics, heading to three locations - Grand Cayman, Cozumel, and Cancún. It was also a 7 or 8-day cruise. I also do not want to give the impression that the qualification to be a top producer was an easy task. It was nothing less than hard work. To achieve any level of honest success, it takes knowledge of your products, work, consistency, and fortitude. When I say work, I mean pray first. Then you have to day after day, acquire leads, work your leads, make calls, keep calling, set appointments, give presentations, answer questions, drop by if you are in the area calling first, until the answer is yes.

By consistency I mean staying with what works without diverting because of feelings coming into play, which throw off one's focus. Fortitude is the ability to keep going when a sale is lost to a competitor, or a presentation is not your best. You must stay on course. Every presentation may not be flawless, sometimes you blow it. I do not consider myself being above average in intelligence, compared to the next person. Many would agree with me who know me. I know a lot of people who are smarter than me but are morally and ethically lacking in their thirst to excel. I'm not saying I have always done the right thing in life. No one can make that boast but Jesus. Considering this fact, we all should strive to do the right thing and overall maintain a sense of integrity in character and practice.

When we fall short it should be acknowledged.

We docked at Georgetown, Grand Cayman and came ashore. The buildings were in immaculate condition, well preserved. Tourism and finance are the major industries of the Cayman Islands. The island is a popular resort due to its physical beauty. It also has a great climate averaging around 80-degrees year-round. We surveyed the shops, and spent time walking around the town, after which we returned to the cruise ship to venture to the next location.

Our next destination was Cozumel an island in the Caribbean Sea, approximately 10 miles off the eastern coast of the Yucatán Peninsula, Mexico. We spent some time browsing the retail shops and food areas. After which we returned to the ship to cruise to our next destination. The last location was Cancun which is said to be the heart of the Mexican Caribbean. After wandering through the gift shops, viewing areas of the city, delectable tasting, we returned to the ship to rest up, freshen up, and enjoy an activity or two as we prepared to come home re-energized to qualify for the next adventure. (Review Location Map #2 after Reference Credits).

Chapter 9

A New Opportunity – A New Direction

After returning home from our latest trip, life for the time being was normal and routine. I knew what I needed to do to earn a living and take care of my family's needs. My wife was employed in an excellent job but had to commute a great distance to work by vanpool. Since we moved into our new home our church membership changed to serve in the city where we lived. I had been active in whichever congregation we decided to unite with over the years, and as we became comfortable and the leadership got to know us, my wife and I used our spiritual talents to support the needs of the fellowship. I would teach home Bible studies, work with youth in the church, and occasionally be called upon to give a sermon. I did not know at the time that my life was going to take a dramatic turn over the coming years.

To set the stage as to what took place, I need to reflect on two individual friendships which brought about the change. In my early Christian experience, before my wife and I married, I mentioned the occasions we would have a group study in the home of one of our friend's mother. It is where I met Dewey, as you recall, earlier in my story. The father of a few of the young men attending the Bible study is one of the men that helped to bring about the change. The father was referred by some as Doc, due to having his Juris Doctorate in law. He had an entrepreneurial spirit and a national counseling ministry. As I remember through his nationwide ministry, he was providing a service to churches marketing to them some of the first computer systems referred to as the XT and AT. These, at the time, were the most recent. For frame of reference these computers had 20 MB of information capacity, and the newest one had 40 MB of information capacity. I remember Doc saying every church in his network needed to have the system he was assembling. Doc was a master at his work. I remember buying a system. My father-in-law bought one as well. My father-in-law and I began at the time to explore multiple line telephone systems to market to churches and businesses. We were always looking for good business opportunities. So was my brother at that time. As time preceded the supplier of parts for the computers fizzled out as competition increased.

After this experience I had some business history with Doc, as well as my father-in-law. I do not remember how Doc told me about a person in Oklahoma who was seeking to introduce a new product in the energy field to the U.S., but it caught my attention.

The second person who resurfaced in my life after not seeing him for many years was Lowell, my roommate in college and charitable business partner spoken of earlier. It happened when I was at a gasoline station away from the area where I live and Darryl, Lowell's brother, drove up for gasoline. We exchanged pleasantries, exchanged addresses and phone information. It was not very long before Darryl and his wife, and Lowell and his friend, came to my home for a visit. Well, of course we spoke about old memories, what we both were doing, and said we would stay in touch.

I wanted to know more about the new energy product that Doc spoke about. Doc said he was taking a few people with him to Oklahoma to meet the person with the energy product. I spoke to my father-in-law and we both were on the flight with him to Oklahoma. When we arrived, we were greeted and were shown a cylindrical briquette about 5 inches in diameter and 6 inches in height. The briquette was made from coal. We learned that a Korean inventor operated a plant in his country, but made regular trips to the U.S. The briquette could be lit with a match and was for outdoor use. The briquette, according to the inventor's claim, would burn about 90% toxic-free emissions. The toxins were retained in the ash. There were different burning times for the briquette, fulfilling multiple needs of the user. Some of the briquettes could burn up to 8 to 12 hours. One other fascinating product was called the Lespo, or leisure sport. The product would be used for backpackers hiking when they needed to cook food or boil water. It was a self-contained product housed in a burner made from aluminum. It had legs that folded out from underneath the unit to be set on the ground or other flat surface. It could also be used for emergency energy in the event of a crisis. The Lespo, as I recall, would burn for about 1 ½ to 2 hours. The Lespo was the product that perked the interest of those attending the meeting. The person introducing the product at the time did not disclose his role with the inventor.

The person in control of the product wanted to initiate a private placement and take the process through the stages to an IPO (i.e., initial public offering).

Since Doc, who invited us on the trip, had numerous contacts, the controller of the product and Doc came to an agreement regarding that process which would put a dollar value to the stock of the briquette corporation. This process commenced, and over a brief period of time, state distributorships were being offered.

My father-in-law and I wanted the state of Illinois. We had to develop a plan to distribute the Lespo in the county population centers of that state. As time ensued, we came to find out that the person who had, so we thought, control of the briquette, and the inventor was trying to reverse engineer the briquette. Good was being sought, but once again evil had been attracted. There was great disappointment but contact with the inventor was eventually made. Lowell entered the picture at this time, as one who said he could secure financing. Lowell, Doc, and I met. Discussions occurred. There was a disagreement about the fee to be paid to me for the source of the funding. It was suggested to me what to ask for but looking back it was a bit excessive. Doc and I could not come to an agreement. So now what? Time, energy, and money had been spent toward the venture by my father-in-law and me. A suggestion was made to us by a confidential close source who could reach out to the inventor Mr. Lee Chu Won, who is now deceased. It was considered, and we consented to the offer. The contact source spoke to Mr. Won while he was in Korea. Mr. Won arranged to meet with our group when he returned to California for a visit.

As planned, the meeting occurred at a favorite Korean restaurant selected by Mr. Won in Los Angeles. The first meeting was one about getting acquainted. After what had occurred with the other American, he was cautious. The meeting went well, and another meeting was set. Mr. Won agreed to send some samples of his product to our group. As products were evaluated, we signed a letter of intent to market Mr. Won's products in the U.S. particularly the Lespo. Other locations were also considered internationally. Mr. Won began to share with us various locations which had the type of coal suitable for his briquette.

The type of coal needed was called anthracite; a smokeless coal as compared to bituminous or lignite. Bituminous and lignite coal were primarily used for electrical power generation. The anthracite coal recommended was in Vietnam, and that country was burning briquettes which were in the shape and sizes of Mr. Won's cylindrical briquette. Some, however, were square-shaped.

The briquettes in Vietnam did not burn 90% toxic-free emissions. Therefore, Vietnam could be a country that could use a cleaner burning briquette. As the possibilities were considered, we formed a corporation called H&J Energy Company, Inc. The H and the J were representative letters for Henry and Jennings. My father-in-law was a senior officer of the company, with Lowell being the CEO and I as COO.

As all these things were about to transpire, another year at Presentation Products, was complete, and a trip to Kauai was earned for a week of relaxation and sightseeing. Kauai has the Grand Canyon of the Pacific, Waimea Canyon, which we had a chance to view from a high observation point. The view was beautiful. The canyon is approximately ten miles long and up to 3,000 feet deep. Also, we were able to swim at one of the beaches there. We had to hike through a wooded area to gain access to the beach.

Upon returning to our car, as I entered it, an exotic mosquito flew in. It was captivating being black and yellow. Mosquitoes, and I do not get along. So, you understand what I had to do? (Review Location Map #3 after Reference Credits). The trip would be my last with this company as a new direction emerged, which I felt at the time could be the financial instrument to further spread the word of God worldwide. I also had great hopes of the company securing my family financially in the days ahead. I can remember going to my father-in-law's family, and my family in Chicago, to present to them the opportunity to participate in the briquette venture. Mr. Won had also sent us a video of his plant in Korea, ribbon-cutting ceremony, opening day of the plant, and the assembly line of the products being fabricated, packaged, and shipped. Our families participated financially.

Prior to their participation, we wanted to travel to Vietnam to do our due diligence on the coal articulated by Mr. Won. I decided to remove my profit sharing of nine years from Yosemite waters to invest in the new venture. Lowell had contacted a Vietnamese businessman who would be our translator and guide from Vietnam. The tickets were purchased and the four of us departed. The person had arranged to meet us before the trip at a Vietnamese restaurant in Westminster, California. The dinner served was delicious after Lowell's friend made recommendations according to what each of us had a taste for.

The flight was exceptionally long, somewhere between 16 hours or more, from LAX. I remember some of the passengers moving into the aisles to stretch and walked up and down to loosen up because of the time in the air. We also followed the same pattern. We had a stop in Japan, refueled, picked up passengers with others leaving the flight, and continued to our destination.

As we approached Vietnam, it was evening and we were flying into Ho Chi Minh City, which is also known as Saigon. It would be the first time for me to come to Vietnam, but not for my father-in-law, due to the Vietnam War. He was there in the mid-1960s. The population estimate for the city in 2006 numbered 5,244,700. The city we had flown into was not the city of the coal mine reserves. The coal was north of Hanoi, Vietnam's capital. We would stay overnight in Ho Chi Minh City and get a late afternoon flight to Hanoi. There was a stark contrast in flying into Ho Chi Minh City than when flying into Hanoi. When flying into Ho Chi Minh City we could see the bright lights of the city, and there appeared to be a lot of life and activity below. When flying into the Hanoi airport it was as if we were flying into a remote location, with very little life. It seemed eerie, lifeless, dark. After doing some research, as I am authoring this book, I came to understand why there was such a difference between the two cities.

The civil war between the communist government of North Vietnam and the pro-Western government of South Vietnam started in 1954. The U.S. entered the war in 1961, reasoning if the communists prevailed there would be a domino effect for the other nations in the region.

The Vietnam War brought bombing of Hanoi by the U.S., and over time caused massive damage. We were engaged in war. I am in no way seeking to focus blame on the U.S. during the war, where many of our servicemen lost their lives. I am only answering my own curiosity as I presented earlier. The civil war and U.S. bombings were the cause of the darkness flying into Hanoi.

Upon landing at Hanoi, we went through a checkpoint, showed our identification, carried out our luggage, and caught a taxi to the hotel in downtown Hanoi. The first location had dirt floors in the rooms, so we went to another more accommodating hotel. I remember taking a shower in a bathtub with no curtain.

As Americans we take a lot for granted regarding the conveniences we have, not realizing a great portion of the world does not have our standard of living.

In the morning the street in front of the hotel was busy with activity, pedestrians on foot going to their destinations, the streets jammed with bicycles, mopeds, and vehicles.

Our Vietnamese representative arranged for transportation to the coal producing area north of Hanoi. It would be between a 6 to 8-hour drive. As we were in route and the outlying portions of the city vanished, we began to see the lush greenery of the countryside. The roads were in some spots semi-paved or just dirt and bumpy. When our vehicle stopped at a rest spot, I was, as well as those with me, rather taken with what we saw. There was a concrete structure without a roof with open bays where there was no enclosure for each bay. The bays were where one could relieve themselves, but there was no privacy, no running water, no flushing, and you were visually exposed to the waste of others. This area was like an outhouse with no roof or walls, but on a broader scale which had not been serviced. I wondered to myself if there was some mobile unit that came to these types of stops to clean out the waste? I didn't ask the question and after about 15 minutes we departed the rest stop.

I started to realize that we were in a relatively poor, underdeveloped portion of a communist country.

When we reached where we would sleep, the compound was controlled by the military. All the valuable mineral resources were controlled by the government. It is the way things are run. It was a reality we had to accept if we were going to do business in their country, purchasing a mineral resource from them. Almost everything we did; we were expected to pay for it. Why shouldn't we coming from America? The lodgings in the compound were well kept and suitable accommodations. The evening, we arrived we were offered beer by some of the greeting party. As I have shared earlier, I stopped drinking many years before, so I declined, and the others also, because they did not drink. Unfortunately, the greeters were offended and insisting that we have a drink with them.

The two greeters had already been drinking, so after they expressed how they felt in Vietnamese, they accepted the fact that we did not drink, and we were given sodas. There was no refrigeration in the compound, so we drank room temperature sodas. The beds we slept in had mosquito-nets around them, for which I was grateful. I loathe those blood suckers. I am always the one they come after, and I swell up easily by their bites.

The following day we were shuttled to the mined coal stockpiles. The coal was in multiple sizes - from granular, to nuggets, to huge chunks. We saw how the coal was sized - the workers were using hand picks. We were at a shipping dock for the export of various sizes of coal. We did not go to the actual mines to view how the coal was extracted. We only viewed the finished product we would be interested in acquiring. Mr. Won was right after receiving some samples. The Vietnamese had a good smokeless coal mineral resource. I was able to give a presentation to the authorities from which we would purchase the coal. We had a chance, also, to see the coal briquettes being used by the Vietnamese. The cleaner burning coal briquettes invented by Mr. Won were needed in Vietnam. The question was could they afford the one's produced by H&J.

As we made our way back to Ho Chi Minh City, we were able to sign a preliminary agreement to acquire the anthracite coal.

One further note, I must relay, is that in the hotel where we stayed in Ho Chi Minh City, I was served the freshest, most flavorful orange juice I had ever had in my entire life.... I inquired about it and the waiter told me it was freshly squeezed. A product of Vietnam. I gave them a huge compliment. I would love to procure the fresh quality of that product on a continual basis. Soon we packed our bags and had lunch in a small restaurant. The shrimp was what I ordered, and I kid you not, the eyes were still in the head of the shrimp! Have you ever seen a whole jumbo shrimp after it has been boiled? It may freak you out if you have not had it served to you in this fashion. (Review Location Map #4 after Reference Credits). It was nice to board our flight back to the states, having gained a greater appreciation of the country I lived in. As we arrived back to LAX, energized from the trip we had taken, we started looking for sources of funding. To receive funding from banks and private sources a financial plan is necessary. A five-year plan is crucial for private sources.

Sometime after our return, I accompanied Lowell to a social gathering where we crossed paths with an old friend, Art Simburg. Art, at one time, was the national sales representative for Puma athletic shoe company.

I remember receiving my first pair of Pumas from Art as a basketball and track and field competitor while at Cal Poly. Art had also accompanied Lowell and I when Marvin Gaye invited us to take a ride up to Santa Barbara, to look at a property that produced avocados. Marvin at the time had a large RV, which was used for the trip. Art had a lot of associations, and after speaking to him about the briquette venture, he came on board as our VP of public relations. Lowell and Art established the contacts that would add value to the company and the ongoing funds to keep us afloat as my father-in-law and I formulated the five-year plan to legitimize what our company aimed to accomplish. During our five-year plan development two additional people entered the product picture to solidify the expertise needed to strengthen our proposed plan.

One of them was an inventor of a patented desulfurization process, which had undergone numerous tests. His name was Charlie Simpson. He lived in the Phoenix area and had a residence in the San Fernando Valley area. We, over a short period of time, entered a letter of intent with him.

At this point H&J Energy Company had two letters of intent, which were clean coal technologies, and a preliminary agreement to buy coal from Vietnam to bring a cleaner burning briquette to their country. The second person who would be instrumental in bringing the desulfurization process of Charlie Simpson's to the prospect of viability and industrial use was Dr. Quazi.

Dr. Quazi, is a wet chemistry engineer and had his offices in San Dimas, California at the time. We met with him and some of the engineers he employed and discussed the Simpson desulfurization technology. After several meetings and evaluating the process, Dr. Quazi was convinced the process would work and that a pilot plant would validate his convictions. We were in the process of developing the five-year plan. My father-in-law sat with me for many days, answering questions regarding assumptions necessary for the five-year plan to construct the financials. All were based on projections. Anyone who has gone through that process knows the work involved. In looking for funding sources for our project a certain amount of collateral was needed, which we did not have.

Our project was going to need millions upon millions of dollars to launch. We were doing private placement between family, friends, associates, and referrals. We worked out of our homes to minimize costs.

We looked and looked, and finally a funding source was made available for specialized funding for humanitarian and environmental projects. The company was based in Laguna Hills, California. Our five-year plan identified and supported the need for $100 million in capitalization. In the meantime, another contact was made, which opened the door to the country of China.

His name was Henry Chanwing. He had contact with key representatives in the Chinese government, and through him we would make an exploratory trip to China. In weeks we were on a flight to Rizhao city, in Shandong Province. China has coal reserves, mines their coal, and burns coal in power plants to generate electrical energy. The Chinese also fabricate coke from anthracite coal to make steel. The contacts in China were extremely interested in our clean coal technology to reduce the sulfur dioxide and nitrogen oxide emissions. The first trip to China was to find a site for a desulfurization plant which would be built. Once arriving in the province, and reaching the city, we were brought to where we would stay. The accommodation was adequate for our time there. The Chinese contact of Mr. Chanwing in China was Mr. Zhiqiang, who would be our representative for H&J Energy Company in China.

Rizhao was a port city on the China Sea. We were introduced to the port authorities, looked at an industrial area which had building structures that would house a coal processing operation. As we sat down with the planning commission, we were asked whether we would want an inland location near railway systems or a harbor location for export of desulfurized coal. The city selected was the port city of Rizhao. Mr. Zhiqiang had a tailor take our measurements to provide the visiting guests with some gifts from the country.

After we toured the areas in Rizhao, we headed for Beijing, the capital of the People's Republic of China. (Review Location Map #4 after Reference Credits). Our group was taken to a coal producing mine and a port where coal was being handled by heavy equipment machinery.

After being shown the coal industry production side, we were taken on a sightseeing excursion to the Imperial city, where the moated Forbidden City, and the Imperial Palaces (now a museum) are located. We also were taken to the Great Wall, which was quite a spectacle. The Great Wall with all its branches runs about 4,500 miles east to west, stretching across 15 provinces of China.

After this trip, our team boarded our flight to return to the states with a renewed sense of having viable technologies which would assist coal burning countries to reduce toxic emissions harmful to life and the environment. On our return to the U.S., I met with Charlie Simpson who wanted to do some testing, so we boarded a flight to Lakewood, Colorado. He, in the past, had done some testing in a lab which assisted in getting the patent on the desulfurization process.

I remember Charlie beaming with joy at his chemical formulation because the release of sulfur from coal fines (i.e., granulated coal which was small) was captured in his lab flask. We both were viewing a yellowish sulfur liquid in the flask. The lab gave the test results solidifying the removal of sulfur in parts per million.

The next trip Charlie and I made was to Vancouver, Washington to examine some separation systems, which could be used with his chemical formulation having a combination of vibration with a water mechanism that was ideal for the desulfurization process. Tests were conducted at the company facility which sold the separation systems. We acquired the brochures for the system with all the specification and volume information for pilot plant operation. Around this time, I began to also look for anthracite coal reserves in the United States. I acquired the "bible" of the coal industry, which had all the types of coal, the locations, number of reserves in the United States, etc. - called the Keystone Coal Manual. The resource is packed with geological surveys conducted over time. The names of companies were listed as to who held the rights to the coal reserves, the United States government being the largest.

The research from the coal manual identified two states that still had mineable anthracite coal reserves. Those reserves were in Arkansas and West Virginia. Our intent was to use this type of coal for the Lespo, or leisure sport utility briquette, fuel source. Anthracite was a primary coal source for domestic use because it produces little dust when handled and burned.

It burned slowly, while emitting relatively little smoke.

It contains more fixed carbon (about 90 to 98%) than any other form of coal and the lowest amount of volatile matter (less than 8%), giving it the greatest calorific or heat value. Because of this, anthracite is the most valuable of the coals. It makes up less than 2% of all coal reserves in the United States.[iii] After identifying where anthracite could be found in the U.S., it was our endeavor to determine how it could be acquired.

We came by a name in western Arkansas, a person involved in the coal business at one time in Arkansas. Her name was Barbara Brickey.
She referred us to a person that was experienced in the coal business by the name of Jim. We were informed by Ms. Brickey and Jim that there was an old mining site owned by Mid-America (i.e., a company which mined coal in western Arkansas). There were various property owners adjacent to the mining operation of Mid-America. It was our intent to identify an owner in the same area as the Mid-America mining operation, which had shut down. Lowell, my father-in-law, and I boarded a flight to Fort Smith, Arkansas to meet with Jim and explore the coal region in Sebastian County. I had already researched the Keystone coal manual and found there were anthracite coal reserves remaining in western Arkansas. We met with Jim at a motor lodge, stayed overnight, had breakfast and were off to the area. We came to a few locations that were used to ship coal, which had, it seemed, little activity. The locations inquired about us and were told we were surveying the area looking at properties. I remember Lowell producing an idea about having round ball briquettes for barbecues. His idea was to have Pro-sports figures do endorsements for baseball, basketball, and football. The briquettes would look like the ball used in each sport. I will say more about this as I proceed with my story.

Lowell had a clever idea. In our exploration we discovered a lady who owned a coal property which had been mined.

We had to make a second trip for the proper introduction and to receive permission to survey her mining property. On our second trip, we brought Dr. Quazi. We met the landowner and gained permission to have access to her land, which had a mining operation in the past. The coal seam averaged about four feet high overall.

The land was filled with boulders of all sizes, which could develop into a secondary rock quarry business. The land also had natural methane gas associated with the coal seam. It was determined that a feasibility report needed to be done concerning the economic viability of the coal property. We employed a land survey and minerals specialist professional to construct a report.

The report came back positive, and a letter of intent was signed with the landowner. The finance company out of Laguna Hills accepted our five-year plan and after jumping through some additional requirements we were approved for $100 million USD in capitalization. Our team was extremely excited about this development. I understood, over time, there were approximately 100 projects that were being funded by this company. Before this news came, we took a team to China once again to meet with officials who could establish a business agreement with our company to allow our technology to be used in China. We can remember a grey hue covered parts of the snow due to the electrical power plants emitting pollution from burning coal. Our clean coal technology would address that problem. There was a business conference in Beijing. All went well, and a letter of intent was signed which outlined China's financial commitment and what was expected from H&J Energy Company. As I remember the second time around, we were taken to a fashion show and provided with a lavish meal which had endless entrée servings. One of the dishes provided had a fish of which the body had been cooked but the head of the fish was still in place and the mouth was opening and shutting right in front of us. This was a wow experience for all of us. The only response from our host was that this was an indication of Chinese wisdom. On our final trip our group was motored to the Great Wall, which some in our party had not experienced. Soon it was time for departure to return to the United States, and we again touched down at LAX excited about what had been accomplished.

The idea Lowell had about the round ball briquettes took shape upon returning. A letter of interest of endorsement was put together to reach out to David Falk the manager of various pro basketball athletes such as Michael Jordan, at that time.

A Power-Point presentation was developed for a scheduled meeting to speak about Michael Jordan endorsing the round ball briquette, which would have the resemblance of a basketball for use in the barbecue briquette consumer market. An appointment was scheduled, and we boarded a flight to Mr. Falk's office for the presentation in Washington DC. After the presentation and discussions, Mr. Falk was intrigued by our offer. So, the door was opened whenever our production capability materialized. The next pro athlete approached by Lowell was Sammy Sosa.

Mr. Sosa had three consecutive years hitting 50+ homeruns with the Chicago Cubs.

Lowell was able to approach Mr. Sosa and caught his attention to sit down for discussions regarding his endorsement of the round ball briquette, specifically the baseball replica to be used in the barbecue fuel consumer market. I would handle the paperwork, i.e., the proposals, letters of intent, letters of introduction etc. I remember Lowell arranged a meeting for Mr. Sosa to meet Joe and Katherine Jackson at their home. The Jacksons had a very nice lunch prepared for Mr. Sosa, Lowell, Art, my father-in-law and I. Mr. Sosa, Mr. & Mrs. Jackson, and all of us, spent time socializing after which Mr. Sosa signed quite a few baseballs for the Jackson family. Mrs. Jackson was a huge fan of Mr. Sosa. In a few weeks Mr. Sosa would also sign a letter of intent endorsing the baseball version of the charcoal briquette. Communications had been ongoing with Montgomery Ward at that time, to carry the endorsed baseball product.

Sammy Sosa in 2000 had a birthday party in the Dominican Republic. Lowell, Art, and I were invited, and my wife accompanied me. At this time Mr. Sosa had finished building a new house in his home country. One of the investors from New York was a native of the Dominican Republic. His name was Angel. He was our guide and was of great assistance, having prior knowledge of his country. It was our first time in this country. Angel set up our hotel arrangements, where we would eat, where my wife would have her hair styled, and where we could do some sightseeing in the city. The night we arrived the Hollifield and

Tyson Championship fight of (1996) was shown, which we were able to see in the sports venue of the hotel where we were staying.

The following evening was the night of the party. I remember when approaching the home of Mr. Sosa, the street in front of his home was very wide. As we were walking up to the entrance there was a line of guests extending about 50 feet and moving slowly as Sammy and his wife greeted the guests as they were being admitted. The home was a showpiece as we entered, going up steps which were in a walled compound.

As the guests mingled in the evening it appeared that most had arrived, and therefore an outdoor enclosed area, with all types of finger foods, was made available to the guests.

As the invitees partook of the various foods, music commenced, and those who wanted to dance moved to the patio floor to the tune of various Caribbean samba style music. As the night wore on, one well-recognized guest appeared by the name of Donald Trump, who at this point in my writing is now the president of the United States.

Once the evening festivities ended, we returned to our hotel and prepared to depart the next day, having enjoyed our experience in the island nation. We boarded our flight and returned to the U.S. (Review Location Map #2 after Reference Credits).

Chapter 10

A Peep at Home Life

Before moving on with the progress of the developing coal business venture, I want to pause and briefly reflect on my family life. When my wife was expecting our second child and came home on maternity leave, there were those in our church congregation homeschooling their kids. My wife having taught early on in several Christian elementary schools, we discussed exploring what would be best for our daughter's education. Once my wife delivered our second child, we made the decision that my wife would leave her well-paying job, remain home, and homeschool our oldest, with the intent to do the same with the new arrival. At the time, it was my impression we would be receiving capitalization for the briquette and clean coal project within a reasonable time, basically it was right around the corner, or so I thought. I was seeing blue skies as the saying goes. I was active with my family in our church and community. I had an office in my home with Presentation Products, and this same office would be used for H&J Energy Company moving forward. The arrangement I had kept me close to my family. When my older daughter started playing soccer with associations she developed, a team was formed, and she played in a small city league. At the end of the season the idea of forming a club team with the best players took shape and was established. The team started out in the lowest category, which is bronze, and developed into becoming a silver team. My wife and I were taking our daughter to weekly practice. Our youngest also traveled with us to see her sister going to various soccer fields to compete.

Tournaments were held and we found ourselves going to distant cities such as Irvine, Lancaster, Palm Desert, San Juan Capistrano, and Mira Mar; all primarily in Southern California. The tournaments were typically Saturdays through Sundays. We stayed in various motor lodges when in distant cities. The team and parents ate together, cheered together, celebrated together upon winning, and when losing felt the same disappointment. The farthest distance we traveled for a tournament was in Albuquerque, New Mexico.

We had a great team. What has just been outlined continued to occur for years, to when my youngest started competing in soccer.

Whenever we were not traveling for soccer, or I was home not traveling on a business-related trip, the family was in church worship service and participating in service activities. We also, on occasion, had devotions of scripture reading and prayer in our home.

During summers, for years we were participating in church youth camping trips in the San Bernardino Mountains. We enjoyed pitching our tent, getting our inflated mattresses ready for our sleeping bags, seeing meals prepared for the youth, and watching the youth participate in various games and activities. Sometimes I would have to leave the camp to oversee some business aspects back home and then return by nightfall. At night, on occasions, there were campfires where there were toasted marshmallows and graham crackers and Hershey chocolate to make smores. These were some enjoyable memories with family which also included beach outings. For many years we participated in a home-school network, which had a yearly home-school fair in Ontario, where homeschoolers participated in developing various projects to enter their work to compete for award-winning ribbons. There were also competitive events of running, jumping, and other areas of activity for different age groups. The concession stands had all types of food, baked goods, drinks, and bottled water. Everything was reasonably priced. The home-school network also conducted graduation ceremonies at church facilities around the home-schooled. Our oldest daughter graduated after completing her 12th grade studies and entered college having passed the SAT test. Our youngest daughter was home-schooled only through age 12 or 13.

This story will unfold later as to why. I remember gathering for prayer on multiple occasions, with some of the high school youth and parents at the flagpole at Perris High School, to pray for our youth and nation. One of the members of our congregation, whose name is Charles had middle, high and college school ministries through Bible Clubs on campus. He coordinated these events at Perris High and at other school locations. These were enjoyable and memorable times.

Chapter 11

What's with Our Funding?

After receiving approval for our $100-million-dollar funding, the firm in Laguna Hills was very slow in funding its projects. Early on, I made a bad decision to leave my job at Presentation Products. The primary reason was based on a bad assumption from a close source who was securing earlier funding that predated the Laguna Hills firm, which did not materialize. When I entered the coal venture, I had an A - credit rating and multiple lines of credit. Over time, I was exhausting my credit lines to handle, in part, expenses for the company and my family. When the project was approved by the Laguna Hills company, this opened the door for expansion investment in our project. Many prospective investors wanted proof we had secured the funding. Since the Laguna Hills company was taking a longer time to fund us, it provided our company with a letter outlining our approval for $100 million USD signed by the company president. The letter helped to sustain us. I was considering returning to work, but I was urged to stay on the course because my office work was necessary in providing the paperwork-prospectus to interested parties. I also oversaw record keeping, and phone communication to assist in answering questions via conference calls. We were given estimates as to when the funding would occur, but it always passed the projected date. I stayed in contact with the Laguna Hills funder for updates and was assured the funding was in the final stages of completion. As our corporate officers conferred, we agreed we would need to seek other funding sources as backup. Lowell spoke with an attorney who had given some business counsel and was friends with a funding source in Taiwan. The attorney contacted a bank source. Lowell, and I received word that they were considering our project. We decided to fly to Taipei, Taiwan to meet with the party. Upon arrival we stayed in a familiar setting - the Sheraton hotel - and prepared to meet the party recommended by our attorney associate. The meeting occurred, but for some reason there was resistance, and we sensed that the banking officials once meeting us had no intention of providing a loan for our coal project. The meeting was short, and we shook hands and left being highly disappointed.

Our meeting was a waste of time and looking back, a video conference call would have been a better way to meet and discover whether there was a genuine interest. Hindsight should assist in future decisions. (Review Location Map #4 after Reference Credits).

The world of finance always looks for how the funds will be collateralized, and the return on investment. We needed an unconventional source of funding which would take a reasonable risk with our project.

Upon returning to the U.S., Lowell, Art, and I continued to seek capitalization for the company, as our main source continued to affirm the funding was being put in place. The unfortunate circumstance for us concerning their claim is that it stretched into years instead of months. Many of our investors began questioning the credibility of our funding source, and we could not fault them. We went to the funder's offices in Laguna Hills, and they had not shut down. We were given assurances, but it was told to us that arbitrage financing for us and the other projects takes time to put in place to fund each project which reached into the billions of dollars. Upon returning from our meeting, we sought to assure our investors. Some wanted out, while others remained.

Lowell had been in communication with Joe Jackson. Mr. Jackson was going to Liechtenstein to visit some friends of his, whose son was desiring to become a pop artist. Mr. Jackson, as I remember, had his own record label. Mr. Jackson also wanted to help our situation and possibly open a door or two for us in Liechtenstein. Mr. Jackson, Lowell, Art, and I checked our luggage in at LAX, boarded our flight and headed to Liechtenstein via New York to Zürich, Switzerland. As we arrived in Zürich, we were met by Al, the aspiring pop singer, with a friend of his. Our luggage was loaded into the vehicles, and we traveled from there to our destination. The time of year was winter, sometime in December. The Swiss Alps were in view with partial covering of snow. The highway we took had various highway road systems that bore through the mountains. Looking back, I remember as we drove through portions of Zürich, it was exceptionally clean. The buildings were well preserved, and the people appeared industrious, hurrying to their destinations.

While on the highway I was very much enjoying the countryside, picturesque beauty of the Alps, and wondering what experience lay before us as we motored closer to the country of Liechtenstein. I am uncertain as to the amount of time it took to reach the city of Vaduz, the capital.

I am one who loves scenic drives. My father would take my family on drives when growing up as a kid. The drives would always take us to places that took up the greater part of the day, from the time we would leave in the morning to returning in the late afternoon or evening. Some of the drives carried us into the following day, such as Hearst Castle on the Pacific coast. I still remember the blanket of clouds we ascended above to reach the summit where the castle rested. At that time there were animals on the property from places like Africa. The furthest drive was to Chicago, to visit our relatives for a week's stay. So, I appreciated what I was experiencing, knowing it was a rare and unique opportunity for a person with my humble background, having never been to Europe. When approaching the city of Vaduz, it did not have the skyscraper buildings of New York or Los Angeles or other major business centers of the world. It was more suited as a smaller city even though having buildings up to 10 stories similar in size to let us say, a Midwestern city with a very reduced population. Yet one familiar with the country knew it was a tax haven with banking institutions that control billions and possibly trillions of dollars from people around the world. We finally arrived at the hotel we were to stay at during our visit. I, and the others from our company at the time, did not know that the wife's father of Mr. Jackson's friend owned the hotel we were visiting. Mr. Jackson was given the key to the president's suite, and we were given separate suites of amazingly comfortable accommodation. I remember the view from my window, like a picture from a Christmas card where one morning there was light snow blanketing as far as one could see with icicles dangling from the trees outside my window. It was a unique experience for me, not having lived in a city where snow was commonplace.

Once we had relaxed and freshened up, we were taken for a drive around the city.

While out we stopped at a broadcast station where Al worked. He played some of his recorded tunes of which one, I thought, had the possibility of being a hit. Mr. Jackson, having been in the music industry for more years than the age of Al, was more reserved and thought more work was needed.

Over the course of our visit the husband arrived, having been away being a foreign dignitary in one of the African nations. He was a very gracious man and spoke a variety of languages. Al and his mother continued to be our chaperons, and we were introduced to people associated with the city's industry. Some of these individuals were represented when I gave a Power-point presentation on our company in a conference room in the hotel. One evening, news reporters came to the hotel and had an interview with Mr. Jackson in his suite regarding his trip to their country. We were all present with Mr. Jackson during the interview and when the business of H&J Energy Company emerged, I gave a brief description of our company, its type, and why we were there. Looking back on our visit, it was obvious that very few venture capitalists would invest in a startup venture unless a lot of due diligence is performed, astute experienced management is in place, with assurances of a return on investment. The other factor is someone needs to know someone linked with investment money for your approval, even after that, the I's needed to be dotted and the T's crossed. Another hindsight insight, I personally invested a lot of my time and money in H&J Energy Company to see it succeed, not just for me and family, but for all those who invested their hard-earned dollars as well. I also still yearn to have a company which was profitable, so I could use a portion designated for me to spread the gospel worldwide and further support ministries to which I was already gifting. One evening as we would be leaving the following day, we were taken to Austria, a short distance away to have dinner at a restaurant in a Bavarian castle. I can remember the drive as we neared the location. We ascended the road that eventually brought us to our destination. Since it was evening it was hard to determine what height we had to climb to reach the top. My other thought was what the view would have been like if it were daylight.

As we entered the castle there were shops inside near the restaurant. Once we went in, it was busy with customers dining or sitting, anticipating a delicious meal like we were. One of the dishes the restaurant specialized in was a dish I ordered due to the suggestion and approval of Mr. Jackson's friend's wife. The main part of the entrée was called schnitzel. It was a nicely cut portion of breaded veal, with all the trimmings. It was good. Everyone enjoyed the meal they ordered. The appropriate tip was made and after our social interactions, we departed.

The morning after we had a continental breakfast in the hotel, we were served sliced lunch meats, croissants, cheese, and fruit juice. After packing our bags, extending our thanks to Mr. Jackson's friend's hospitality, kindness, and gracious lodgings, we headed back to Zürich to return to the states. (Review Location Map #5 after Reference Credits).

Chapter 12

A New Company

As we returned to the United States, realizing that no source of funding would come out of Liechtenstein, an underlining frustration became evident which had been simmering for some time between Lowell and me. It became apparent that we could not work with one another any longer and parted ways. Our philosophical and religious differences were diametrically opposed. Looking back, we both had committed a thing or two against each other that should have been taken care of with apologies, but those issues never were resolved. Understanding that life is too short at this stage in my life and being one that knows I will have to give an account to Christ my Lord and Savior, I am expressing my humble apology to Lowell here and now as I write. Also, to all the others that I have disappointed or offended over the years, whether for their financial losses incurred or for any other reasons, I am deeply sorry.

The next thing that occurred was the need to activate a company I had in reserve which I planned to use for another purpose by the name of Tri Energy Inc. After speaking with Art and my father-in-law, each of us committed to making those investors in H&J Energy Company whole regarding what we owed them. Our thoughts were to continue taking every possible viable route available for the new company to finance it to repay the investors and develop a thriving business in the coal industry. Our backs were against the wall with most of our options exhausted for a business startup. Just before the activation of Tri Energy my father-in-law and I needed to go to Birmingham, Alabama to meet with Jim to connect with a coal source owner who mined and shipped coal. Our interest was the need to establish coal mining sources, to supply our desulfurization technique. We met with Dan, had discussions, and could see by the conversation he had been in coal mining and distribution of his product for some time. We were also taken to a port on the gulf, where coal was stockpiled in preparation for shipment by barge to the buyer's various destinations. Cards were exchanged, and Dan would be a coal source for our clean coal processing venture.

As time continued to move forward, one of Art's associates referred him to a person that had diplomatic ties, had been in international symposiums, and knew heads of states in various countries.

The person's name will be kept anonymous in my story. You will later be able to connect the person as a would-be financier of Tri Energy, Inc. I decided not to dignify this, because he caused great harm to our company and investors. Multiple years have passed without our project funding. Every source or possibility always seemed to end with no commitment other than what was received from our Laguna Hills funder. We continued to put our heads together and recognized the urgency to establish a revenue stream to repay our investors. The thought surfaced to explore the possibility of establishing a coal mine operation. I believed after doing a considerable amount of coal industry research, our company should begin mining coal and selling directly to those coal consumers needing a higher BTU bituminous coal product with low sulfur content. I called Jim and asked him if there were any locations that could begin a coal producing operation in a minimum amount of time. He told me he would investigate my requests. In a few days Jim got back to me on a conference call with my father-in-law and Art. Jim had a contact source in Virginia, where he could arrange to meet with us.

The person's name was John, and he was located in the southeastern portion of the U.S. where there was a plentiful supply of high BTU coal. My father-in-law and I decided to fly to meet Jim's source after our discussions in our inner circle. Once the meeting occurred and the possibilities were shared, we let John know we would be back in touch with him after speaking with Jim. Once we spoke with Jim, he decided to join John to establish a coal producing operation. There were mining leases available in the eastern portion of Kentucky. Art had a building contractor who was interested in participating in our upstart mining operation. Art and I took a flight to El Dorado Hills and met with the contractor and his wife. The meeting went well and soon after, Tri Energy was being capitalized for the mining operation upstart. As coal assets under lease by our company increased with millions of tons of reserves, the value could be established for the company.

A website was set up with the information provided for interested investors to research our mining permits, coal reserves, and coal product mined at our site.

I made available a prospectus for investment, to dig ourselves out of a deep hole created over the years. We were always of the belief that we could set things right, make our investors whole and manage all the regulatory issues related to securities. If we had stayed with coal operations and continued to provide updated equipment to increase production progressively, we possibly could make good on our commitments.

Unfortunately, the person referred to Art by one of his associates would take us for an unrecoverable ride, which we would regret for our lifetime. We were seeking good but attracting evil.

Chapter 13

The Infamous Gold Deal and Coal Venture

The infamous Gold Deal agent was referred to Art by one of his associate's. The phony agent supposedly was well connected with heads of state, involved in international symposiums, and persuasively lured us into a story with the appearance of legitimacy. The question is how did we let this happen? The individual presented himself as a mandate, or agent for a gold transaction between one country and a prince of another country. The agent presented to us that once the transaction was completed, he would receive $1.2 billion USD. When we visited his offices, they had the appearance that he had connections as expressed. We saw pictures of dignitaries and heads of state, and plaques of symposiums he was in, which gave a degree of credibility. Over a brief period of time, say months, the individual spoke of the closing of the gold transaction, and the need to make payments to various agencies and persons, which could delay the finalization of the transaction.

When his need was presented, I developed a proposal with the help of our mining office, for seven more coal properties with lease availability. I put together all the new equipment needed for the present coal operation, the equipment for the seven-mine expansion project, the debt incurred from investors at the time, and a projection for a future amount which came to be a sum of $200 million USD. Four copies were made of the proposal/agreement between the officers of Tri Energy, Inc., and the gold agent. After his and our review we all signed the agreement. After that time, Art was to stay in contact with the agent for updates and needs, while I stayed on top of the mining operation, banking deposits, transfers, investor communications, and paperwork. My father-in-law kept records of investors' participation and amounts of return. Art also led the communications with investors and those wanting to invest. Art would three-way me into investor calls to provide an overview of the mining operation. As time continued our company would have group conference calls to minimize three-way calls. The conference calls could accept up to 99 people to be updated twice per week. On Sundays we had a prayer call.

The agent of the gold deal would also occasionally give an update on the gold transaction. The investors were aware that the gold transaction had costs, so they participated, but we had to secure them through the coal mining operation. The unmined coal reserves under lease had a value. Each unmined ton had a value of between $1.25 to $1.50. When you have millions of tons under lease, you can calculate the unmined coal reserves asset value which gives the company that value. Tri Energy had three coal mine leases with an unmined value of over $10 million US dollars.

We later found out that our fourth lease was falsified, which was uncovered by a new superintendent of the mine because Jim had some civil issues in Alabama and was incarcerated. This revelation happened further down the road, but looking at leases, I thought I should mention it here because I was unaware of its fabrication, having been sent the agreement to add to our coal reserves. The discovery would put in question the amount of coal Jim said had been mined at other coal sites under lease. An investor could go on-line to verify our control of mining permits and review pictures of our operation at our website. Other things at the mining office were discovered, which I will share later. The fourth lease, which was fraudulent, had us under the impression we controlled over $22 million in coal reserve assets.

The agent continued to need more funds to close the gold transaction, but the funds going to the agent caused our mining operation to suffer. We could only afford used mining equipment, which kept needing repair parts, so there were delays in coal production. If it was not a continuous miner breaking down (machinery that cuts into the coal), it was a shuttle car (a coal vehicle transport), or front-end loader or something needed on the conveyor belt taking the coal up to the surface from 1,200 feet at the base of the coal seam. We had to make sure the miners/laborers were paid, and workers compensation was paid quarterly, or we could not operate. The mine had inspections from OSHA - Occupational Safety and Health Administration and MSHA - Mine Safety and Health Administration.

These agencies could shut down mining operations if not in compliance. Also, there was a constant flow of water from an aquifer needing to be pumped continually to keep the mining operation from flooding.

More than one pump was on site but both needed parts to continue to operate. The other costs were a royalty to be paid to the landowner each month while we mined coal. I was in direct contact with the controller of the coal property. There were times when we did not mine coal over several days, due to breakdowns and as a result, we did not meet our production quotas. The mine was not profitable due to the older equipment and repairs. All the revenue from coal sales was going back into the mine. I was given projections on what our mine would produce, but those estimates could only be realized if we had steady production. Another issue, which was unforeseen in the mine at the time, was mining into rock. When this occurs, the continuous miner needs to be reset at another place along the seam for the coal to be more accessible to mine. The reset takes time. Sometimes the seam of coal can be up to 6 feet in height in this mine, but in some places, it can be a foot and ½. So, you are not only mining coal but also dirt and rock. Coal mining may appear to be a cash solvent venture with lofty expectations, but there are unforeseen hardships which occur, especially for one who is new to this type of business with equipment issues. The operators at the mine were experienced, but I had to rely on their input. With all the concerns at the mine, we still had to stay the course to remain operational and help the gold agent to the finish line to receive our funding. I met a finance professional much later, when it was too late, who shared with me our coal reserves value could have provided the funds to lease or purchase mining equipment. If so, that was our answer. It did not come to mind with all the distractions. My error. Our Laguna Hills funder was not out of the picture. We met with an international insurance company, which would be the instrument to distribute our funds of $100 million in monthly installments of $6.25 million per month for 16 months. There were issues involving the moving of substantial amounts of funds into the U.S. because of the 9/11/2001 incident. As you remember the terrorist attack on the Twin Towers in New York.

The Patriot Act was put in place, and it was an exceedingly difficult time for the movement of large funds, due to money laundering linked with terrorism, etc. Once my father-in-law and I met with the vice president of the insurance company, we signed off on what would occur. We were not given a day or time. Within a few months leading to the date in early January 2003, I received a letter.

It was what we had been waiting for, for years. The letter indicated that our project was the recipient of $100 million USD. It had the bank from which the funds would originate a funding/bank code number and the increments to be received. When I saw the name of the bank, it was a well-known European bank, and the date of disbursement would commence on March 3, 2003. I felt my prayers, and all the others who had been praying, had finally been answered. I began to contact my business partners to give them the news.

A call came about two weeks or so later that the FBI had raided the offices of our funder in Laguna Hills, confiscated all the computers, five-year plans of all the projects, and shut the company down. I felt as if my heart had been torn from my body. I knew because of the length of time it took to fund the projects, some of the projects went to the authorities with complaints. All the projects paid retainer fees to the Laguna Hills company. There are no further words that I can articulate which can capture what I was experiencing at that moment. All the time, work, the waiting, to end like this, shattering the hopes for everyone involved. What more can be expressed? I had to recuperate very quickly and continue moving forward to reach the goal of funding and paying out the investors. With the expectation from the agent of the gold deal, which we thought would close any time, we were going to need more buyers for our coal product. One of the managers whom we had flown to meet initially in Virginia, knew a representative of coal consumers and wanted us to meet with him. The representative was in New York City, staying at the Waldorf Astoria Hotel. I let our representative know that I would get back to him as soon as possible once arrangements were made to fly to meet the coal representative. I spoke with Art and my father-in-law about the possibilities, and we all agreed that a sit-down meeting with the prospect would be appropriate.

Since it would be my first time to New York, Art and I contacted Angel who made arrangements for us in the Dominican Republic to let him know my father-in-law and I were flying into his city. I alerted John when we planned to arrive and to call the coal representative. Upon our arrival Angel picked us up from the airport and we were on our way to the Waldorf Astoria Hotel. After getting settled into our room, we contacted the coal agent. We met in his suite. It was apparent he was doing business from his room. He was an older man and appeared to have been in the coal business for a long time. We talked about our company and what we were attempting to accomplish.

Afterward, he shared that there was a coal need in Italy. He told us the type of coal, its specification, amounts, and asked if we were able to provide a product? If so, the door would be open. The negotiation of price per ton would come into play when we were ready. The meeting did not last long. We made the contact, exchanged business cards and we parted company. After our meeting, Angel took me and my father-in-law to a Brazilian restaurant. I heard that New York was a great place for food. The food we had was great, multiple portions of various types of meats brought to our table, a buffet style self-serve food bar for the side compliments. It was my first experience in this type of restaurant. After the evening dinner, we were scheduled to leave the next day. We were in and out and on our way back to California, having gained an agent as a buying source for our coal product. The information was made known to our supporters. We continued to support the closing of the gold transaction, even to the detriment of our own mining operation. As time continued, we learned that Mr. Lee Chu Won had throat cancer. He was a cigarette smoker. His cancer eventually took his life. We were very saddened by this occurrence. Our contact who opened the door to meet with him gave us this news. The inventor Charlie, of the coal desulfurization process was up in age, but the wet chemistry engineer was confident the process would work having understood the process. The issue was capitalization for the pilot processing plant, which we did not have. All our original plans had to be altered to center on acquiring coal leases and mining coal to sell to move toward meeting our financial obligations. The difficulty in meeting the coal projections was a constant need for parts to keep our mining equipment operative.

Our agent of the gold transaction continued to say the deal was close to closing, but another financial issue needed handling. Therefore, monies that could put in place newer mining equipment which would increase our production, were going to the agent. The best being done at the mine was constant repairs, which caused the missing of our mining projections month after month having a substantially lower production. Every 90-day projection took into consideration the gold transaction being closed. It would mean new mining equipment installation, with the expansion of more coal leases. Mining permits put in place would increase coal production to make our company financially solvent and pay back our investors.

These things were our expectations. Our mine superintendent and engineer thought the coal production projections given to us by them were realistic. The two of them thought the projections could be reached with the equipment they had. The two of them were mistaken, due to the variables in the coal seam as explained earlier, and due to shrinkage in height and solid rock formations. There is no type of x-ray machine that can preview the contents of the coal seam. By not having this preview bred optimism. If someone produces an invention of that type, well you know the answer. The mine I am speaking of was named Pine Creek, near Mayking, Kentucky.

I came to learn our other two leases were not mining coal. Early on Jim represented that one of them was producing coal. As time continued to elapse, some of our investors wanted their money back because of the length of time it was taking for the gold transaction to finalize. When investors want their money returned, you have two options. 1, return their money, or 2, try to talk them into waiting a bit longer. Some were able to hold off after speaking with them, and others could not be persuaded. If our mining operation is not breaking even for the reasons already mentioned, where would we get the money for those who were insistent on wanting their money returned? I will take it one more step. What if they tell you if you do not return their money, they will contact the authorities. We knew if that occurred, we would have to deal with that distraction, and eventually be shut down.

We also knew the only way we could fix our legal predicament was to get our funding and pay our investors. What would you do? Let the whole venture collapse, or try to finish what was started for all those concerned? It was a wrong decision to take money coming in, to comply with those wanting out. It was a decision we regretted then and would regret later. Even with the best of intentions, there are still regulations the company must abide by, and when those rules are violated, there are consequences which will bring shame and disgrace. Some companies have survived having broken some rules, but others have not. Tri Energy was headed down the road of the latter. Plans not materializing as projected brings doubt, and all types of accusations from various investor participants. I would feel the same way if I were in their position.

In early 2004, we were visited by 10 of our investors. We met at Art's home, had discussions and it was decided to confront the agent with the gold transaction. We prayed before we left. It was a short ride to his office not too far from LAX. When we converged on the agent's offices, he was at first nowhere to be found. After our search, he was found hiding under a desk. The agent more than likely thought we were there to engage in physically attacking him. However, we were there for straight answers. After we all calmed down, we sat in his office in silence at first. Comments began to be made by those who had come. The agent was called a fraud, and a liar. He responded by saying, "The gold transaction was still alive." After continued discussion, some of the investors had spotted a restaurant across the street from the agent's offices. Art and I decided to take a break and have a bite to eat with investors. In the discussion some were under the persuasion the agent was not legitimate - a fraud. Others had no definite conclusion, and one thought he did have a gold deal. Once Art and I met to decide what should be done, we were torn both ways but decided to continue to believe the agent had a gold transaction. If we had broken off from the agent and focused entirely on directing funds into the mining operation, we would have had a reasonable chance of recovery, but we chose to remain and finalize the gold transaction. The prompting of a few investors encouraging us in that direction. Others gave us a warning not to pursue that course. The latter counsel proved to be right.

As time wore on, we were able to keep the mine operating and producing coal but were still below production projections. Other avenues were considered to capitalize our coal venture, as we waited for the gold transaction to finalize. We were still diverting monies to the gold agent.

We maintained large group conference calls to update the investors. We had those conference calls recorded for those who missed the updates, for them to access them at their leisure. The gold agent would give periodic updates. Our new coal mine superintendent, because Jim was incarcerated, began to disclose to me that coal sales were not in the name of Tri Energy, but in another name. The news was highly disturbing, because now we could not trust our former mine superintendent. Just by alerting me to the fact that the disclosure came from the new mine superintendent lent credibility to him. Marty was also the one who told me our fourth coal lease was fallacious, because he knew the owner. The copy of the mine lease with the forgery of the owner's signature brought more sorrow.

The information regarding the forged lease was stated in our prospectus, about five or six months before my discovery of it being a fake lease. The investor pool was already on edge, so I said nothing about the discovery and extracted it from the prospectus going forward. It was another wrong decision on my part. The concern for the gold transaction, the situation at the mine which occurred, the investors needing to be made whole, kept me awake after going to bed. I sensed the roof crumbling and the foundation breaking up, with Tri Energy in the middle. What was occurring was irreparable unless the gold transaction closed. As I reflected on how the funds were being dispersed, which came in through investors, our mindset was to continue to minimize our personal expenditures, to keep the operation of the mining of coal afloat and finalize the gold transaction. Art and I were both driving early model cars. Art a '93 Mazda and myself the '92 Honda I mentioned earlier. We did not feel deserving of any items beyond what was of necessity until we could be in the position of making our investors whole. We wanted to cross the finish line having made good on our promises and commitments.

I remember constructing a termination letter listing the violations incurred by Jim and was ready to get it notarized and sent to the mining office but held back with him already being in jail for a civil issue. I regret not conducting what would have been a normal exercise to officially terminate him, but at the time everyone knew in the mining office Jim could not return. I let it go having only given a verbal. The notarized termination letter with Jim's false representations, could have been of future assistance in my upcoming case.

Chapter 14

Company Collapse - That Fateful Day

I knew the heat would come, due to those investors who were convinced the gold transaction did not exist. Also, we were not registered to issue securities in any of the states. Everything expanded very rapidly, not having the time to provide the legal fees to register in every state where investor monies derived. We thought we could fix these areas once our funding arrived. First, the state of Washington's, securities department subpoenaed us to court, followed by the state of Montana's, securities department that did the same.

As time continued, we heard from the U.S. Securities and Exchange Commission, requiring us to cease and desist. We had to retain an attorney to help us respond to the commission. We did not use the investors' funds, but a close relative of Art's handled the attorney fees. The attorney we had told us we needed to cease and desist our fundraising activities, to which Art and I committed sheer stupidity on this one. We reasoned that to stop everything would collapse all the hope of the investors which would crush them, and it would be over for the mining operation.

Many of you might be wondering how a Christian minister gets trapped into such a quagmire, becoming involved in breaking securities laws and sinning against the spoken Word of God, which states – "Be subject to the governing authorities." Romans 13:1? My answer: "By thinking God understands and moving forward even though inside you know it's wrong." Those of you who are Christians know we can still do some horrible things in our walk as we progress towards spiritual maturity. The ones looking in from the outside do not realize Christians are not perfect but are under the impression we should be - which is unrealistic. They do not know there is an internal battle occurring between the new, spirit-renewed self in us, and the sinful, fleshly self. Being a follower of Christ is a progressive journey, starting as a child spiritually, and developing through the stages of life towards spiritual maturity.

We stumble sometimes willfully, ignorantly, or by being broadsided, never reaching perfection in this life with our sinful human selves, tagging along.

Christians are to strive as best as possible, doing good, observing God's Word, and letting Christ be formed in us. But we blow it sometimes. My story in part reflects blowing it.

Being a Christian is the most challenging life to live. It is a struggle. Courage is needed, because the world is headed down stream, which is as easy as floating on an inner tube, but we swim upstream, against the current, which is more difficult. What am I saying? In general, it is easy to go with the flow of immoral things from the world's standpoint, which is sinful due to the rebellious nature of not wanting to be restricted by rules. We should resist that direction and come to Christ, where we know it is expected of us to live and abide by His principles. Our attitude overall has been changed by the second birth. Just having that internal conviction confirms we genuinely know the true and living God for He is without sin being holy.

Despite our bad decisions, we have the promise from Jesus Christ, forgiveness now, and the hope of a perfect-sinless-transformed-eternal-nature and body in the life hereafter. Being forgiven, however, does not extend to believers a license to deliberately commit sin and think there is no consequence. If there is no sensitivity to sin or guilt, one must check whether they are truly in the faith. One day the believer will leave behind forever the sinful fleshly self which is corrupt. The new or second birth is available to every human being.

Art again spoke with the gold agent, and he said the transaction should be closing momentarily. Our fundraising activities continued in violation of the United States Securities Commission. Art and I were totally caught in quicksand, sinking rapidly, wondering whether there was a gold transaction. As time went on our attorney removed himself from our case. I began to realize we had been taken. There was no gold transaction.

A short while after that, I had a knock at my door.

It was two FBI agents who asked me a few questions. After a few questions, one FBI agent told me I should get a lawyer. The inevitable was about to happen. We were fools having believed in the so-called gold agent. We had been taken for a ride that would seemingly destroy our lives as we knew it. I had violated legal regulations.

Looking back, how did I allow myself to get there? We had the opportunity to step out of the ride we were in but made irresponsible decisions to remain in the car. What was about to come would bring hurt and hardship to my immediate family, embarrassment to my church family, hurt to the extended biological family, surprise to those who knew me, and overall loss in general to the majority of the investors. We had been seeking good but attracted evil people who had no care for anyone other than themselves. I must also say that my sinful decisions in violation of the Word of God were evil. God did not make me do anything that violated His word, which is on me. God is good - all the time. He lays out principles in which we are to abide by, and when we do not, we reap the consequences. If it appears, we have escaped some consequences this will occur only by God's mercies (i.e., not giving us what we deserve). My sinful inclinations moved me against Him. Thank God for Jesus, my eternal Advocate who died for all my sins - past, present, and future.

The fateful day came when the doorbell sounded early one morning. There was an assortment of people at my door. One person, a U.S. Marshal, asked who I was. After my response, he then asked me to step outside the door and as he frisked me, he then handcuffed my hands behind my back. My wife and daughter were looking on, my wife telling my daughter to remove herself. The FBI, the U.S. Postal Inspector's office, and the Sheriff's Department were all present. As they walked me down my driveway to a passenger van, the door was opened and I was seated, then transported to downtown Los Angeles to the Metropolitan Detention Center (MDC).

As we rode in the van I could not help but feel defeat, disappointment, and helplessness. How could I rectify the harm I had caused?

All the promises made, effort exerted, hopes and expectations of those who believed in us, who would suffer monetary loss because of us. I remember looking into my wife's eyes before leaving, there was disbelief, disappointment, and the fear of the unknown. I believe I said to her it would be all right. But it was not going to be all right when the process concluded. Art was also picked up the same morning. The gold agent, we came to understand, had flown to Hong Kong. After he was tracked, he fought extradition. Eventually, a U.S. Marshal picked him up after being detained by the local authorities.

I had a chance to speak with my sister the same day I came to MDC, and she posted a bond for me, so I was out the next day after my hearing. I was not a flight risk, so I had my freedom for the moment. When the indictment came all our accounts associated with Tri Energy, Inc., and H&J Energy Company Inc. were frozen. Also, any sole personal account I had was frozen. I had to have my house appraised to release the bond paid for me by my sister, so my house would be encumbered for $80,000. I had consulted with my wife about taking a loan out on our home to help close the so-called gold transaction. She was against me making that move for the fact of me exhausting all my profit-sharing from one company, and all my credit cards for trips not only for myself, but the officers of our company. Her "No," saved me from having to be detained before trial because our home at the time had not been encumbered. Eighty percent of the equity in our home had to be available to post a bond. I had to find work while I waited for my trial date.

I was offered a plea bargain by the prosecution. I would have to say I intended to defraud the investors, which would have been a straight out lie. So, I turned it down. However, Art being up in age was offered a plea bargain, so to reduce his time he consented. He had to do, what he had to do. I am not mad at him. I forgive him. However, I was disappointed. The public defenders representing me said I did not have to say I intended to defraud investors, but something along those lines would be sufficient. But how does one get close to that admission without saying it? I was told by my counsel to think about my family. I did want to spare them a lengthy sentence if I were to lose. My counsel said it would be difficult to win the case if I went to trial.

If I cooperated, I would probably be sentenced to eight years, if not the U.S. attorney could seek the maximum time for the alleged crimes. I did provide a typed statement of what I felt I could admit to, but I was told it did not go far enough.

I decided to go to trial, because to spare myself the possibility of getting double the time if I lose, was better for me than to betray the trust of the people who invested in our company with a lie. I put the outcome in God's hands. The trial was not for about a year and ½ or so. I was able to find work and continued to support my family. My wife also sought work and had to suspend the homeschooling activities with my youngest daughter. All of this hurt me as well as them.

Over the period of my working, the prosecution was putting together their case against me and the phony gold agent. I had to fly to Sacramento to sit in on a deposition of one of our investors who handled the recordings of our conference calls. The investor and I were both told that we could not converse, so we greeted each other, and nothing further was permitted. My counsel from the public defender's office accompanied me. All the while awaiting trial, I was wearing an electronic tracking device around my ankle. I showered with the device, ate, slept, and went to work with it fastened to my ankle. No one knew as I went from business to business, location to location, that this device was strapped to my ankle. My sales territory took me from Riverside County to San Bernardino County, to Los Angeles County, and to San Diego County. I was given permission to go to these areas by the pretrial officer I had to check in with before and during trial. My trial commenced in the last week of June 2007. It took 11 days. I was advised by my counsel it would be better for me not to take the stand to testify. It was indicated to me that the prosecution's skill at cross-examining me could work against me, rather than for me. The only way that certain pieces of evidence could be shown as exhibits in my defense was if I were to take the stand. This was a dilemma for me. I began to realize I was going to be at a disadvantage. Another issue was that the jury instructions were not balanced but were tipped toward favoring the government. The annoying reality to me was that the phony gold agent and I were going to be tried together. I had to sit by this person as if I colluded with him.

I wanted a separate trial, but I had no power of decision in the matter. The jury selection process decided who would be a part of the jury and who would be dismissed. During the 11-day trial, I would leave my home to take the Metro rail from downtown Riverside to Los Angeles then have to walk at a brisk pace to reach the court room by 8 AM. My counselors for the trial told me I had gotten one of the toughest judges in the Central District Court. I began to wonder if there was anything occurring that leaned in my favor? I was naïve to the entire process, and the legal gymnastics of the U.S. attorneys to position themselves to make it almost impossible for the defendant to win his case.

The times on the Metro rail coming into Los Angeles for the trial caused me to reflect on where all of what was happening would lead me. I wondered was my life over.

I wish I could have a glimpse of what was ahead, but no one can see the future but God. So, it is a matter of taking things one moment at a time. I wondered about my wife and girls. I knew that I had to put all my concerns in my Lord's hands and remain faithful to my commitment to Him no matter what. I had to step down as a leader in my church and provide a verbal statement as to my bad management decisions and where my actions led me.

Finally, when the jury was in place, trial proceedings commenced with opening arguments from the prosecution and the defense. My pastor would be a positive testimony in my trial, but one other from my congregation would testify for the prosecution. As church treasurer she could verify my signature. There were three couples who lost money from participating in Tri Energy Inc., and one widowed fellow believer. Each one of the four groups were a part of the leadership team. My family and I continued to serve in the same congregation we were members of for over 12 years. The congregation was very supportive overall. During the trial we were still participating in the service activities, even though my role was diminished. There was an outpouring of love, which was very encouraging to me and my family, even from other Christian fellowships in the community in which we had joint Sunday evening services once per month. It was made known about the predicament I was in. In one of those services the people of God gathered around us and prayed for me and my wife.

It was a very comforting occasion.

As the trial continued day after day, I knew it would not go well for me when the judge made a statement that I was just as culpable as the so-called gold agent. I sat back in my seat and said to myself, did the judge really think what he just said is true? There was no way I could ask him how he could reason and communicate such a thing, with the evidence being to the contrary. All anyone had to do was see where the money went, and for what purpose, to decide about culpability. There are things that did not come out in the trial. But the weight of what occurred was placed on me being the president of the company and signing off on the designated transfers. I was not alone in making the decision to transfer monies to the supposed gold agent's account. I will say no more on that other than I was complicit in those decisions, even to the harm of our coal mining operation.

I am responsible as being the chief officer of the company, and in this case a rather naïve and dumb one, but not one intending to defraud. I had a good faith belief in the gold transaction, if not, I would not have made the transfers.

As the trial progressed, the pseudo-gold agent testified almost creating simultaneous laughter in the courtroom. It was he who used over $21 million for luxury cars and limousines, purchased properties, started a record company with our investor money, signed recording artists, produced recordings, and the list goes on. He tried to prove he had a gold transaction. The prosecution and jury sat in disbelief about what he said. As the deliberations continued witnesses took the stand, some for the prosecution, and a few on my behalf. It came time for closing arguments, and afterwards the jury made their decision regarding our case. As the spokesperson for the jury handed over their verdict, it was stated that a few of them had to make a hard decision. It's unlikely for those few to have in mind the pseudo-gold agent in deciding the verdict. The U.S. Marshal handed the presiding judge the verdict and both the gold agent and I were found guilty of wire, mail, and securities fraud. I had support from church and family attending the proceedings, whom I was able to greet after the conviction as we left the courtroom. The phony gold agent was taken back into custody.

The date was set for the time of sentencing which would be more than a year later November 18, 2008, due to rescheduling conflicts. I was still free to continue working and earning a living until that date finally arrived. I did not know if I would receive the maximum I could receive, or the minimum in the range of my conviction offense. For some reason, I did not eat after Monday evening of the week of my sentencing until after the sentencing had been given by the judge on that Friday. It was not something I planned. It just entered my mind. When I arrived at the court, the other person being sentenced that morning was Art. When the court was called into session Art was summoned before me and was sentenced to nine years having cooperated with the authorities. It appeared he was hoping for a lighter amount of time, but the judge was not to be swayed. The judge explained why he was giving Art the amount of time set. One of those reasons he stated was that I did not do what occurred on my own. Another reason was given, but I prefer not to include that in my story. The judge did grant Art's request for the location of his placement for incarceration.

I was up next and when called my public defender stood with me. I had drafted a statement that I wanted to read before I was sentenced. After my public defender read the statement, she gave me her consent to read my letter of remorse for what had occurred in the venture and the loss of life. When the prosecution was asked what their position regarding the time, they recommended 12 years. The time given to me by the judge was based on the directive from the prosecution.

I had no idea at the time what I could have received, until years later while incarcerated. I read the sentencing guidelines which showed 17 ½ years as a minimum to 21 years as the maximum, primarily due to the pecuniary loss which raised my points. The net loss to investors was an amount just over $28 million USD. Of that the mining operation received a little over $3 ½ million USD. Art received – over 3 1/2 years just over $500,000 based on the prosecution's court presentation. Of that amount, Art had to pay back some hard money loans, etc. I received over the same period of 3 1/2 years - just over $250,000. The remainder of $28 million was paid out to investors if my memory is correct. The so-called gold agent as noted earlier received $21 million.

This is all public record. The presiding judge also instructed both Art and I when we were to report to the prison facilities where we would be confined. We were given the date of January 12, which gave us both the freedom to spend the holidays with our families before reporting to our respective prison locations. I contributed the time I received to the hand of God, because it could have been much more time given in my sentencing. The phony gold mandate received 20 years.

I'm also grateful to the prosecution for not sentencing me to the minimum in reference to the guidelines. My counsel came to me in court on the day of sentencing and explained to me that, with good behavior, I would serve 10 years, five months, and 12 days. As I write this book, I am coming up on my ninth year. As I look back, I can understand what God wanted to do with my life while incarcerated. I will reveal those things as I progress through each location of which I have served time. God also has watched over my family with church and family support through some very tough times without me being home. I will not minimize what I have put my family through, by me being removed from our home. I never want them to experience what they had to go through again. I will try to express what they experienced later in my story while I was absent.

Each one, if they care to, can explain what their fears, challenges and hardships were without me there. I was advised by my counsel to report directly to the facility of my assignment, because if I reported to MDC, it may be some time before they would transport me to Safford in Arizona. My pastor volunteered to drive me to my prison location accompanied by his wife and one of his daughters. It was about an 8-hour drive one way. The 8-hour drive caused me to reflect on what a disappointment I was to my God, my family, and the investors. I felt my days of effective ministry were over. I had the thought that I would arrive at where I was going, and just do my time. I felt disqualified to do any ministry. I thought about how old I would be upon release. My life was at the lowest depth and darkest time with no indication of ascending above my circumstance...

Chapter 15

Incarceration in Arizona

I arrived at what is called a low security facility in the Bureau of Prisons, which is Safford. The complex was encircled with barbed wire except for the entrance. Inside the reception area it appeared the facility was well kept, and clean. I gave a final wave to my pastor and family and reported to the intake officer to start doing my time. I had to change from my street clothes to the clothing of every inmate. After intake log-in as to who I was, a photo was taken of me with a height measurement behind me. I was issued a registration number, which I would be identified throughout my time of incarceration. I received my ID card, and I was set to enter the population. I was given sheets and blankets and assigned to sleep in a relatively new part of the facility called Ocotillo. I was taken to my bunk on the second floor and met with whom I would bunk. I was gradually filled in on when there was a count time, when all inmates needed to be at their bunks, when eating times were, shower times, the politics related to where to sit, what TVs to watch, when Christian services were as my faith was expressed, controlled moves on the yard where you need to be in your workplace, chapel area, or class, or in recreation or back at the living unit. When the time for movement occurred, it lasted for a 10-minute duration to arrive at your destination. There was structure to your movement around the yard. You are expected to abide by the rules, or there would be consequences for insubordination. You could be given a shot, which went into your record of conduct, i.e. (post sentencing info or PSI), or you could be thrown into the Special Housing Unit (i.e., the SHU), which is like solitary confinement. The prison authority could ship you out for whatever reason to another facility further from your home, or because you were in danger due to something you have done to an inmate or inmates. The inmates had a code of conduct among themselves. If you are hot, i.e., a snitch, and turned against the co-defendant you should make that known. If you do not make it known and were found out, you are ostracized, or you may have to check yourself into the SHU. If you were a child molester depending on what security level you were stationed, the inmates could attack you. The highest security level for federal prisons is a Super Max, then USP, then a Medium, then a Low, then a Camp - as the lowest level of security.

There were various tables in the dining hall where one could sit. The races were pretty much divided, so you had to sit with your own people. Sometimes there were exceptions. Each group had a shot-caller who would mediate between disputes associated with a different race, as well as within one's own race. Most of the time things would be managed peaceably, but on rare occasions they would not. On one occasion a person of one race incurred gambling debts across racial lines. He could not pay his debts. He was addicted to gambling, so the shot callers conferred, the debt was paid by the race of the one who had the debt, but the person had to check himself into the SHU.

The shot caller for the Blacks came to me one day wondering how I was feeling about being taken for all the millions that was loss. He asked if I was bitter and wanted to get even with the phony gold agent. I told him no, I was not bitter, and I had forgiven the individual. I could not let what he had done destroy me on the inside. Internally, this is what Christ my Lord would have me do. On occasions, though, I could not help but think about the damage he had caused. I did not know at the time that inmates investigate who are among them. They want to see if a person is lying about his case or telling the truth. Well, after this discussion with the shot caller I was told there was a newsletter from Bloomberg circulating around the compound which had Bernie Madoff, Enron, and Tri Energy named, which was dealing with our loss of investor monies and some particulars about Art and me in the story, as well as the supposed gold agent. I never saw the article. Around the same time, I received letters from the television program Dateline and the TV station MSNBC appearing to be sympathetic to my case. Both wanted to interview me to get my side of the story, so I spoke to my wife and told her about who contacted me, and she asked me not to correspond with them. Her position was there is enough publicity and embarrassment to the family, so more exposure would be even more hurtful. So, I consented not to move forward, and I did not respond to either.

I mentioned earlier, I thought my ministry was over and I would just do my time. The day after I arrived in Arizona, I had to go to the medical for a routine checkup as a new inmate.

While there, I was in the waiting room and one other person was also there. Somehow, we entered a conversation which lasted for about 45 minutes.

It was after that conversation; I sensed there were men on the compound who needed spiritual help. During that 45-minute span no one came into the medical facility, and no one came out to call either one of us.

"What are the chances?" I thought to myself of that happening where there are nine hundred or so inmates on the compound? I still wanted to be used by God but felt unworthy. After spending time assessing my life and the things that led to prison, I poured that out to God. I already knew he had forgiven me, being a loving God who saved me through His Son. I believe I was given the green light to move forward with the ministry where I was. I met and spoke with other men of faith, and sensed they needed to grow spiritually. I asked my wife to send me the 29-lesson Christian Bible study course I developed for the church congregation that I attended when home. The studies were topical and dealt with subjects and issues regarding the Christian faith. Once I received the studies, they were photocopied, and the Bible study group was underway with a small group of six men. Once the study was finished, I started doing one-to-one studies with men who missed the group study. I also realized I needed to find other biblical studies for the men, but did not have access to them at the time, so we started a weekly study in First Thessalonians. There was a volunteer pastor who came in on Wednesday evenings. I participated in his group with about 12 other men. I needed to sit under sound teaching, as well as be accountable. I attended Sunday church services and went to a small group study led by Philly. I spent some time programming, which was mandatory. There were adult continuing education classes, business technology, and vocational classes. For exercise, I walked about 3 miles five days out of the week, played bocce on occasions, shot around on the basketball court, and played volleyball.

The facility at Safford had a sewing factory under Unicor – FPI (Federal Prison Industries) which is designed to operate at a zero-profit. Unicor had contracts with other federal branches of government and supplied the prison system with various items. Unicor had the best paying jobs for the inmates. Our facility made jumpsuits for the Navy and Marine Corps and knit style laundry bags for the inmate population. When I started in the factory, I was laying out the patterns of material which would be sewn together to make the jumpsuits. After a short time, I became a trimmer.

I used an electronic hand-held cutting unit to trim the excess threads left from the jumpsuits. It was not too long after that, I was selected to be a quality assurance inspector. I had a station where I would examine the garments and measure them to make sure they would pass specifications. After that I was moved to the finishing table to fold and box the garments, and seal and stack them. On two occasions I was bitten by spiders and had to go to the medical facility for treatment. There were many ways a spider could bite you when working in the factory. They could hide in the garments being handled, they can be under tables, in bins where garments are placed, and it goes on. Sometimes, you do not really feel the bite, because of your focus on your job. The spiders that bit me went up my pants leg. One bit me on my hamstring - high up, the other above my knee. It was painful the way the physician's assistant had to extract the poison using a razor blade, cutting an x into my flesh where the bite took place deep enough to press out the poison. After all the pressure applied for extraction, the area was cleaned out or disinfected with iodine. Each time it took about 7 to 10 days before the wound would seal up and not leak.

As time moved on, I was able to see men invite Christ into their lives. We had a strong fellowship of believers, and on several occasions one of the brothers would prepare us great meals. We would all buy what was needed from the commissary, and Del would use his gift in preparing burritos, sandwiches, and desserts. Del loved preparing food with a little help from his brothers. As time progressed, I sensed the need to assist the brothers in developing some guidelines that they could use to help them live out some principles of conduct which could be posted in their locker and reviewed daily.

I named this single sheet, "The Believer's Prison Creed." The prison creed can be viewed in the Exhibits section.

There was an inmate at Safford who was a big help in assisting those qualifying to go to a camp, as a transfer from Safford. He was eligible to go to a camp, but for some reason the case manager and possibly higher ups in authority, were attempting to keep inmates at Safford for 18 to 20 months, no matter if they qualified for camp or not. The inmate filed a BP-10, which was an appeal to the region that governs over federal prisons in its district. The inmate explained if he were to get hurt at Safford when he should be at a camp, he would hold the Bureau of Prisons responsible.

The Region responded very quickly and ordered the authorities who made the decisions to transfer anyone who was eligible for a camp to process their paperwork and transfer them as soon as possible. The region, by doing this, affected my transfer, because I had been at Safford for almost 15 months. Anytime one drops under 10 years, including good time, and had ten points or less in their PSI they are to be transferred to a camp. My paperwork was processed, and I went to La Tuna camp in Anthony, Texas by furlough (i.e., without escort). The town driver for the facility drove me to the bus station after I said my goodbyes to the brothers, and I was off to my next location by Greyhound bus. The Greyhound bus made other stops on the way, but finally arrived in El Paso, Texas. It was about a 6-7-hour drive. There was nice scenery traveling across several states. The first leg of my time of incarceration had ended, and I now would experience the lowest security level facility in the Bureau of prisons. Sometime later, it was disclosed to me that a riot broke out towards the end of the week I left Safford.

Chapter 16

Incarceration in Texas

Upon my arrival in El Paso, I had to take a taxi to the camp, it took about 30 minutes. When I arrived there, there were two recognizable facilities, a low security facility and the camp. One had the appearance of a castle surrounded by barbed wire on three sides. The other was open with some fencing. I had the taxi driver drive me to the camp but there was no activity in the administration offices of the camp, due to it being after 6 PM. I was driven up to the Low, or the castle. When entering there was a reception area, and an officer behind an intake module with protective glass. I told him I was reporting from Safford to go to the camp. I gave him my ID. After running a check on me he said my processing to enter the camp would be done in the morning and I would have to sleep there overnight. An electronic security door opened, and I was escorted to the SHU.

The SHU is not a place you want to be placed. This was my first experience in the SHU. The castle was an old facility, so the SHU was not a comfortable place to sleep even for one night. It was dirty, had ants, and roaches, and a thin mattress laid on an iron surface which did not give. There was no pillow. The SHU was a place to discipline inmates. There was a tray with some food remains, which was a reason for the multi-legged crawlers. Other inmates were in the SHU, but I was separated and put in a cell alone. There was a book in the cell that I had no interest in reading. I had a thin blanket in the cell, but no sheets. The cells had a solid door, and clear opening that could be seen through with bars, and a place in the door to receive food trays. There was no other visual outlet in the front part of the cell, or the surrounding walls. There was a sliver of a window, whereby some light may slip through during the day. It was so small, to prevent any thought of escape. The lights were controlled by the prison. All I knew was that I wanted the night to pass quickly, and my release from this whole experience to pass. Now I understand the reason the SHU has an alternate name, which is the "hole." When morning came, I was taken to a holding area to be processed to enter the camp. It was there that I was given something to eat.

In about an hour I was taken to be processed to go to the camp. The camp (the lowest security facility) was about ¼ of a mile from the castle. Once I was driven to the camp, I received customary items, change of clothing, boots, undergarments, socks, sheets, and blankets. I met the inmate I would bunk with, and two other men staying in the same cubicle of the dorm with two bunk beds across from us. This was the overall arrangement throughout the dorm. There were two housing units that housed approximately 150 men each. One was on the lower level of the compound grounds, the other which I stayed in, was on the upper level. Between both facilities there was a quad area with grass having steps and sidewalks encircling the sloping area. There were paved areas for wheelchair access. There were many full-grown trees inside the quad area, as well as on the outside of the compound. Each facility had a counselor and case manager's office, restrooms, and showers. There were three TV rooms. Swamp coolers provided our air conditioning, being an older facility. There was some wildlife in our area, such as road runners, rattlesnakes, squirrels, rabbits, and all types of birds. There were also a host of cats that had adopted the camp. The cats were semi domesticated overall and could be found lounging in certain parts of the area on the side of the lower dorm where there was a narrow pathway that took one down to the athletic facilities. Every now and then some stray dogs would upset the tranquil atmosphere the cats enjoyed, by chasing them. The cats would escape easily having the trees to resort to. There were no mice to be found around the facility grounds, due to the cats. Just outside of the area where the dorms were, a basin lay where tall grass grew from the rain drain off. A bridge was over that area. It could be seen in the distance, which would handle the traffic in both directions. A waterpark was near the facility, due to Interstate 10 highway being about two hundred yards or so away.

My bunkie was an older man similar to myself, but in his early 70s. He was a very nice man, and financially well off. He taught a class on trading in the stock market. He was a trader and had done very well. It was unfortunate that he came to prison. It was not anything related to his trade. But I am not at liberty to state the reason for his incarceration. It is too sensitive. The bunks everyone had were made with old-fashioned down mattresses, with springs that had flexibility.

It was a more comfortable sleep than at Safford, where I tossed and turned due to the iron frame and surface with a thin mattress to lay on. I was assigned to the kitchen for my job duties, specifically the dining room and beverage bar. I would mop floors, clean tables, make coffee, mix flavored drinks, and prepare the ice water. I participated in the Sunday church service, attended Bible studies led by an inmate named KC. I met quite a few Christian brothers.

As the needs came up, especially for the inmate services which took place on the fourth Sunday, I had the opportunity to deliver the message. I also used the 29-lesson Christian growth course with a sizable number of men. There were a few men who came to Christ during the time at La Tuna camp. I was still in need of more studies, so I searched the chapel to see if there were studies, I could use.

On one occasion, when I was in the chapel, one of the inmates came through the chapel door, saying that I was on a television program. I paused and thought I would go and investigate what was being represented. By the time I arrived, I was only able to catch the last 10 minutes of the program. What I learned was that the program was on MSNBC - called American Greed – "Fools Gold." I knew this would be a nightmare for my family. It is exactly what my wife did not want. What we hoped would be laid to rest after my imprisonment was now being broadcast nationwide. I remember speaking with my father, who was called by a few of the members in his church about the program being aired. My brother also told me he viewed the show, which really cast me in a bad light. I began to wonder whether I should have accepted their invitation to give my side of the story. It was too late for that to happen at this point.

When I was not working, or participating in studies of the Scriptures, or viewing something on TV, I continued my exercise routine, which was primarily walking. On occasion, I would do some exercises with some weights to strengthen my arms, primarily curls with dumbbells. I also shot around with the basketball. There were some younger men who ran full court. I was invited but declined because the surface was concrete.

I did not want to start down that rode again, even though it was tempting. My mind was saying to give it a shot, but my body told me my glory days were over. As a compromise, I played some of the men in basketball games, such as horse or around the world. I won some games and lost a few. As time continued, having worked at Unicor garment factory at Safford, I had priority over others at La Tuna to get the job when an opening surfaced.

I was soon able to leave the dining hall and started a position at Unicor due to an inmate's recommendation named A.J.

There was a vast parking lot of government vehicles needing various alarm systems, emergency decals, blinking lights, reinforced bumper bars, and other parts. The Unicor at the camp handled the receiving of what needed to be installed on the vehicles that were warehoused at our site. The things ordered by Unicor from the Low/castle were put on pallets, cellophane wrapped, forklifted into a flatbed transport vehicle, and delivered to them for installation. I kept track of inventory coming in and going out. Also, I participated in stacking each item on pallets, pulling them from inventory by forklift or hand. We also had to double check that every item ordered was on the pallets. The four-man crew took turns mopping the warehouse and helping with inventory audits, along with their own responsibilities. One of the bonuses working at Unicor was a fruit garden planted outside the warehouse. The fruits grown were cantaloupes, watermelons, and a few other things such as grapes and tomatoes. The vocational training and business training classes were about ½ a mile from the dormitory and administration areas. Every year there was a harvest of pecans that grew on the extremity of the federal property. The pecans, when ripe, would fall to the ground and were collected by those authorized to be in the area. The Authorities did not want anyone collecting the pecans to eat, but for obvious reasons it was not observed. The clean-up crews were to collect them and discard them. To let the nuts rot, I suppose, would drive the men nuts. There were inmates who had confectioner's experience and made candies, and other assorted goodies out of the pecans. Some were unshelled and eaten raw, being ripe.

I was amazed by the creativity of some of the guys who transformed something simple like pecans or other things from the commissary that made enjoyable, tasty eating.

I want to take the time to share about the deep and valuable loss to me of my mother, experienced while at La Tuna camp. I was notified by my sister, who had been caring for our mother before I entered prison. She fought for her life in a gallant way, having contracted breast cancer and had radiation and chemo-therapy treatment. She had to have a mastectomy early on. My mother was the best mom a son could have. Always there. Always in your corner. Always loving you. Always helping when the need would arise.

The camp officials were approached about furloughs home to attend funerals of loved ones who had died. One inmate only wanted to go 60 miles away, and one other 300 miles away. Instead of the furloughs being granted, they were denied. The authorities to prevent any leaving of the camp due to grief, placed both men at different times in the SHU. Every inmate could not understand the rationale behind confining men in the SHU, when they are already emotionally distraught. This all took place right at the time my mom passed. When my sister asked if I could support the family emotionally by attending the funeral, I had to explain what had been occurring at the camp. The men were assigned to the SHU for 7 days, during the time of each funeral. If the other two men had not asked for furloughs, I would have asked unknowingly and landed me in the SHU. They would have asked me the date of the funeral and would have locked me down for 7 days, until the funeral was over. My distance to come home was much further than the other men. So, I had to keep quiet and grieve alone regarding the loss of my mom or be confined in the SHU. I also lost an uncle and a stepmom while incarcerated. This is another reason, or incentive, for one to stay out of prison. You never know who will die. I disappointed my family because I could not be there to offer my hugs, and my shoulders for their cries.

The politics in the camp still had shot callers for each ethnic group, but seating in the dining hall was not strictly observed.

There were TV rooms controlled by the Blacks, Hispanics (primarily due to sheer numbers), with Whites, Native Americans, Islanders and Asians having some input. Anytime disputes came up among the races, the shot callers would control their own people and resolve any conflict as at the Low.

During my stay at La Tuna, a few fights broke out that were among their own race but did not involve the whole compound. Overall, the stay at La Tuna was a peaceful one. One day while in the TV room some men were being challenged to do some push-ups which caught my interest.

I had not been personally involved in doing push-ups in my exercise routine. Someone asked me to do 20 push-ups. At first, I declined and then reconsidered to give it a try. When I got to 10 push-ups, I started having doubts I would make it to 20. One person said he will probably do about 14, another said maybe 16. I was really laboring to get to 20, so I got to 19 and could not push out one more push up. I felt embarrassed that I could not do 20 push-ups. One person said, "Oh Robert you can't do 20 push-ups?" I decided that I needed to add push-ups to my exercise routine. I started doing push-ups and got to 20 push-ups and went above 20 progressively. I started doing sets of 20 push-ups and increased from there. Yeah...

I was still in need of Bible studies for men that had gone through the 29-lesson course. It was laid on my heart to develop some questions and answers regarding the commands of Jesus Christ to his disciples in the Gospels. I started with Matthew and finished that book, and then tackled Mark. After finishing Mark, I did the same for Luke and John. There was only a legal typewriter at this camp, and no computers with accessible word processing capabilities. All the studies from the Gospels were written out by hand in a question-and-answer format. I am not a fast typist, but if I had a computer, I could have formalized the studies. I stored them away until the day I could put them into a Word program. I began considering laying out studies in the letter to the Ephesians, but here again they were handwritten. My studies were evolving, and I did not know to what extent at the time, but God had in mind for me to develop Bible studies.

As the work regarding Bible studies became a focus for me, an opportunity was made available for me to get closer to home in California. A work cadre program was being made available for those who wanted to assist in opening a new federal prison in Mendota, California.

I went in immediately and requested to participate in the program speaking with my case manager. She began processing my paperwork for transfer, which was approved. I arrived at La Tuna in May 2010 and would be transferred from there in December 2011. After wanting to remain in California after my sentencing to stay closer to my family, I believe it was God's will for me to experience the two facilities I did some time in. Each location gave me the opportunity to minister to men that came from all over the nation. When one is a part of God's spiritual family, circumstances beyond one's control are orchestrated by the One who loves him or her. Each location gave me the opportunity to grow spiritually and exercise my spiritual gifts.

I learned some things that can be utilized in ministry, to assist the people of God find their area of ministry. I was handed by one of the inmates whose name was Wes, a spiritual inventory system that could assist believers in discovering their spiritual giftedness.

The combined time at Safford and La Tuna was approximately 34 months. When anticipating my departure from La Tuna, it was said we would not be given furloughs to travel to California. We would go by way of being shackled in chains. When looking back on the way the inmates were transported, it reminds me of the 20s through 50s when there were roadside chain gangs. I was on a very uncomfortable trip to California. The time came for my departure from La Tuna, and I gave my farewells to those in Christ and others with whom I associated. All my belongings were boxed up at the Low to be shipped to my destination in California. Another episode was ending and another opening. I began to wonder what experiences were ahead.

Chapter 17

From La Tuna to Mendota

The inmates who would be making the trip had their hands put in the chain apparatus that went around our waists and linked into a box in front of us. We had very little movement of our hands, and the cuffs around our wrists were tight. The next security chain shackled our ankles, which gave little play between the right and left ankle. Each ankle was put in cuffs like our hands. The picture I am trying to describe is like the prisoner (Alex Montel) in the orange jumpsuit in the movie SWAT, with Samuel L. Jackson. What was almost impossible was stepping up to the step on the bus, due to the limited length of the ankle chain from one ankle to the other. Since the chains were iron, the weight causes the ankle cuff to press into each ankle area it surrounded. The officer could adjust the tightness when first putting on the wrist and ankle cuffs. However, metal of that type was still aggravating and painful. Being transported in this way should be one of the deterrents to returning to the prison system in my view. When our bus started out, we had a limited number of men. As we entered El Paso, we made a stop at a county facility, which added some more men. Other stops were made along the way at other places. We stopped at Big Springs (a federal institution) adding others from there. The bus came to Lubbock, Texas, home of Texas Tech University, where we stayed in a city jail overnight. It was a great relief to be unshackled, to shower and use the restroom without being chained. If you had to go to the restroom on the bus as we were in motion it was difficult to urinate, being inhibited with hands and legs having minimum movement. I personally had to use the toilet standing and with the bus moving and bouncing it didn't go entirely where it should have gone if you catch my drift. The following day we resumed our journey to the Oklahoma transit center. One U.S. Marshal was stationed on the bus in a compartment in the back with shotgun and side arm. When we needed to eat, there was packaged food consisting of wheat bread, peanut butter, strawberry jelly, small packet of pretzels, and cookies. There was an alternate food package with bread, baloney, cheese slices, mayonnaise, cookies, and a small pack of pretzels.

We finally arrived at the transit center, with a full bus load of 40 inmates resulting from all the stops. We were put in a holding area after walking down a long corridor. We were processed in and moved to the housing units on various floors. The building had multiple floors where inmates were detained in cells awaiting transport to other locations. It was a few days before I was flown to Apple Valley, in California, and then being driven a short distance to Victorville. The few days spent in the transit center in Oklahoma were accommodating. We were provided hot meals for dinner while there. Many of the men walked around the enclosure on our floor. Others were exercising, while still others watched TV. There was a time that we would be locked down overnight, and in the morning released into the activity zone for meals, leisure (i.e., TV watching or reading), and exercising. The facilities we were in were clean. The transit center seemed to be relatively new, maybe no more than 5-6 years in existence from my visual assessment. The person whose cell I was assigned to was from Maryland. He did a lot of exercise. I was told when I arrived that the food was decent, as stated earlier. The time came for my departure and the others who would be flying to California. It would be almost 3 years since I would return to my home state. I would finally be closer to my family and looking forward to visits. Since it was the month of December, movement of inmates slows down, due to the holidays. As we arrived in Apple Valley, and were driven to the Victorville prison facility, I wondered at what point I would arrive in Mendota to the camp. Once we arrived at the prison facility in Victorville, we were placed in holding units, which held up to twenty or so men.

When in the holding unit I noticed a person shuffling around, talking to the men of Hispanic descent. There were some places to sit but most had to stand. Suddenly, a commotion broke out with three Hispanic men attacking another Hispanic man. All were still in their chains, yet they were kicking, hitting with hands chained, and the lone person being attacked just crouched to the floor to protect himself. As a result of the noise, correctional officers opened the holding unit and removed the one being attacked. What I learned of what had happened was that two rival gang members were placed in the same security unit.

The authorities always sort through the profile of those being transported to ensure the opposing gang members were separated. Somehow, this was overlooked in this instance.

All the men on the flight were going to different levels of security from a USP down to a camp. At Victorville there were two holding units, one was unit B, and the other Unit A. Unit B was a security holding area for those going either to a camp or to a Low. Unit A was a security holding area for those going either to a Medium or higher level. I was processed in and given my clothing for Unit B and assigned to a two-man cell, which had a double bunk bed, one above the other, a toilet, and sink. I met the inmate whose cell to which I was assigned. The inmate informed me on how things worked in Unit B. The showers faced the open area where men played table games, walked, conversed, and exercised. Unit B was two levels. Both levels had showers above the other. The shower doors were see-through and made of thick wire mesh, so you had to place clothing over the shower cage you were in for privacy. Shower slippers were issued to the inmates, along with towels, soap, and washed one-piece jumpsuits. On the second level were cells that were accessed by stairs, a walkway that ran around almost the whole of the upper level, with railing overlooking the first level. There was one TV on the first level for the whole unit that was elevated ten feet or more. As I met other inmates, learned their names, where they were from, and where they were going, I made connections. I also met with some Christian men who were having prayer every evening on the second level, which I joined. A few of these men were going to the camp at Mendota, so we became more acquainted. I remember having the opportunity to lead two men to Christ, one was going to the camp I had just come from named Tim, and the other was going to Lompoc. His name was Jerome. I was able to explain what Tim had in store for him at La Tuna. Tim was physically fit and asked if La Tuna had a weight pile. He was glad to hear that it did. I spoke to him about some of the brothers to look up, who would assist his spiritual growth, some of which played basketball so he would fit right in. Others familiar with Lompoc filled Jerome in on his destination. We committed all the men we met in our prayer group with others to God and His plan for their lives. We had some Bible studies, and before too long we were spending Christmas in Unit B in Victorville.

I had a visit from my wife and girls, who I had not seen but twice since being out of California. We had a good reunion and conversed about what was happening in their lives.

Three days after Christmas, I found myself shackled and chained again, boarding a bus to be transported to my destination, with another 39 men. Leaving the Victorville facility, the bus headed north through the high desert. We saw hills, cactus, tumbleweeds, and sparse indicators of dwellers living near the route we were taking. The same arrangement of a U.S. Marshal with shotgun was inside in the compartment in the back of the bus; a normal procedure for transporting federal prisoners. There were prisoners from both Unit B and Unit A on the bus. It was evident by some of the comments and stories being told on the bus. The trip to the first location, which was Mendota, took about 5 to 6 hours, with a stop at a convenience store for the Marshals to purchase what they needed and rest. As we came near to Bakersfield a lot of land was being farmed to produce all types of fruits and vegetables. It was the central area of California known for producing a great deal of the nation's produce. I remember coming to this area as a kid. The area was one of the places my father had driven us to with my mom and my other siblings.

Once we made it to state highway 99, we passed city after city until coming to Fresno. After coming to the exit that would take us to Mendota, we merged over and took another 35 minutes or so to reach our destination. The city of Mendota was very small, but was known for agricultural products such as cantaloupes, cotton, barley, corn, cabbage, lettuce, etc. When approaching the prison facilities, it was apparent that the site had a vast amount of federal property. On the property were two facilities, a medium security prison with three separate housing units, each of the units were multiple stories. The administrative unit was one story. All the medium facility was surrounded with two sections of barb wire rising approximately 15 feet or more. The other facility across the parking lot and street entrance was the satellite camp, which was all one story, except for the warehouse and maintenance buildings. The medium's facility could house up to 1800 inmates, I was told, while the camp had a 128-bed capacity that was increased later.

The federal property had other buildings, such as the powerhouse, food, clothing, and other items warehouses, maintenance building, training center, gun range and its small building. There was a large, elevated water holding tank on the property.

The camp's administration building included offices for staff, a conference room, visiting room, patio, medical and dental, classrooms, chapel which doubled as a multipurpose room, computer room, recreation storage room, computer room for GED testing, commissary, barbershop, clothing issuance room, bathrooms, kitchen, dish room and dining hall. The living quarters had steel or wrought iron bunk beds, a small library, two TV rooms, showers, restroom, three staff offices, clothing washroom and wall pay phones. Behind the dormitory were the outdoor recreational facilities.

Basketball courts, a baseball diamond, soccer and football field, volleyball area, handball courts, and track for running or walking were all there. Another area near the track was for ping-pong, horseshoes, and bocce. Over time all these areas were made operational but not when the camp opened. When we arrived five of us were processed in at the medium to enter the camp, others were going to the medium. The remainder of the bus occupants were headed to other facilities such as Atwater or Herlong. It was a relief to finally reach the destination at Mendota. This site would conclude the remainder of my prison incarceration experience.

Chapter 18

Early Days at Camp Mendota

When we entered the camp, we were greeted and given a care package from the Christian church ministry. The items in the package were things we could use immediately, until our property arrived, or we were able to go to the commissary. The items were shower shoes, deodorant, toothpaste, toothbrush, toothbrush holder, bar soap and holder, lotion, shampoo, coffee cup, spork (i.e., combination of fork and spoon), and a shaving razor. We were told the items did not need to be returned, but if we wanted to contribute and help others needing the same help when they arrived, it was our choice. The camp authorities issued us clean bedding - sheets, blankets, towels, and underwear the day we arrived. The following day we received our clothing, socks, and boots. There were close to eighty inmates in the camp. I met some of the Christian brothers, as well as others who filled me in on how things worked at the camp, and where things were. The first job for me at the camp was on a landscape maintenance crew, laying and spreading rock dumped by a front-in-loader near black tarp at the Medium, which had not opened. We arrived on December 28, 2011. I was in Victorville for 21 days. All new inmates had to go through orientation and medical screening before being released to work in the area assigned. After these were completed, I began work at the medium facility. The facilities officer issued wheel barrels, shovels, rakes, and gloves to the crews working the grounds of the Medium. There was preliminary work needing to be done, such as pulling grass and weeds in preparation of laying the tarp. The process went on for two months after my arrival, before the work was finished. Others had been at the camp as early as five months prior. The Medium opened some days after completion. In late February or early March, I was assigned to a new job in the dorm, as a dorm orderly. I dust-mopped floors, mopped, and maintained the dorm area. There were also times when the whole dorm work crew was pulled together to deep clean the facility, due to an inspection, which was coming from a national accreditation agency. The agency would have several types of inspections, some yearly and others every three years. The food was good at Mendota and was in satisfactory portions.

For opening a new facility with the work that had to be done, food was a great incentive to the workers.

In federal prisons the earnings monthly vary greatly depending on where you work. The town driver and commissary workers are the highest paid, outside of Unicor, then warehouse clerk, maintenance clerk, vehicle mechanic, head cook, powerhouse workers, HVAC (i.e., heating, ventilation, air conditioning), and head dorm orderly. The positions named would be Grade 1, however the top grade would vary at Mendota ranging from $60 per month to $125 per month or more. Grade 2 would range from $28 to $40 per month. Grade 3 from $15 to $22 per month. The lowest Grades are 4 and 5 paying $5 to $12 per month, depending upon the work assigned. Some of the men are dependent on what little they receive per month from their jobs, having no outside financial support. Many men have been abandoned by family members. Some have gone through separation or divorce. The strain being incarcerated puts on family, I can say personally, is devastating especially from the loss of my income. The pressure put on wives and children can be loss of home, the sense of abandonment, and feeling of hopelessness and deep hurt. Embarrassment is another factor. My family members were victims of my bad management decisions.

My wife and daughters would be considered as primary or direct victims. The investors who lost money would also be primary victims. The secondary victims have a close relationship with the victims. My family was impacted physically, financially, emotionally, and spiritually. The removal of me from my family impacted them physically. I was no longer at home. I no longer could see them face-to-face daily. I could no longer handle simple repairs around the house, paint, cut grass, clean up the yard, drive my daughters to wherever they needed to go. I could not help solving immediate difficulties experienced by my wife and daughters because I was not there. I could not participate in trips and the list goes on. The monetary loss of my income was crushing. Had it not been for extended family support, my wife and daughters would have no place to live that they could call home. Without my financial support of the family, where will the money come from to deal with household expenses of food, home, utilities such as gas, electric, phone, water, and trash pick-up?

There were clothing issues, auto maintenance, and auto insurance. Where would enough funds come from to handle all these issues? Adding to the dilemma for my wife and daughters was the emotional loss.

Earlier, I mentioned some areas of emotion which would surface, but I did not go far enough beyond hurt, hopelessness, and sense of abandonment, which are real.

The emotions of anger, resentment, distrust, and confusion are also a reality when a husband and dad is removed from the home, due to incarceration. The last area is the one identified as spiritual. While in the home, if you represented your faith by action, and demonstrated characteristics which show there was genuineness in your profession, the family should hold firm as to who you are. However, when the unexpected occurs, such as being incarcerated, a seed of doubt can work its way into an unsuspecting heart diminishing the credibility one once had or saw in the spiritual leader of the home. When coupled with the absence of the incarcerated from being home, it is very difficult to influence the direction of the household. The one to blame is the one incarcerated, having left home with all four of the issues represented. I love my family and understand my errors of poor judgment have caused what my family is experiencing today. I will say that God has brought them through exceedingly difficult times, since I have been away, with the support of other family members' sacrifices, for which I will always be grateful. Our church has also been helpful. I also can say I have had continual financial support from my sister and father to help me through this difficult time. Others have wanted to send support, but I owe others and feel undeserving to receive from most of those I disappointed. My pastor, and the church I was a part of, have sent many Bibles into the camp, which have been a blessing to many men needing the word of God. I have had good prayer support from relatives and friends which have gotten me through this experience. God has kept me busy, participating in His work to build disciples of Christ for His glory. As I'm writing this book, I am approaching my sixth year at Mendota Camp.

I had no prior inclination in my heart to write about my life's experiences. I did not think I had the where with all to write this book. I heard of others who were incarcerated writing books. Some have asked if I thought of writing a book, and at the time, I had not thought of doing one. During this year, two fellow inmates said I should write a book because I had an interesting life to tell about. After the two men suggested, I remember several others in years past, said the same. I thought how embarrassing my story would be as a Christian.

I have been imprisoned. Furthermore, I always thought I needed a large vocabulary and had to be a professional writer. I decided to try it and see if I could make a difference in someone's life in a positive sense and keep them from the heartache of my negative experiences, and if so, then it would be worth it.

I also felt the Lord was giving His consent. I asked for His assistance, "He said He would never leave me or forsake me." Hebrews 13:5. He was there all the while when I was not listening or heeding the governing authorities, and when I reaped the consequences.

God has taken me further than I could have imagined. He has laid things on my heart, that apart from Him, I would not have attempted. The Lord has caused me to redeem my prison time. The hours and days have not been wasted. I have had very exciting experiences by the gentle prompting of the Holy Spirit, but the carrying out of those things was not easy. I have been pushed and challenged beyond what I thought could be accomplished. Jesus' attitude was to do the will of Him who sent Him and to finish His work. John 4:34. My passion is to do the same, no matter how meager I may believe it to be. I am put in awe of His grace, mercy, love, and forgiveness that has been given to me, despite me. The gifts and calling of God are irreversible. Romans 11:29. He can pick anyone up, clean up him or her, and use one for His purpose if one is willing. God is a God of second chances, and I am thankful He is that kind of God, and most assuredly has demonstrated this in my life. In Proverbs 24:16, in part it states, "For a righteous man may fall seven times and rise again." It is Christ's gift of righteousness received through Him. He makes one righteous by transference, I do not earn it, but this is how He now sees me and others in Him.

So, we may fall numerous times, but we do not stay down, rising again by His strength living in us to do the right thing, and complete what He has called us to.

As I became adjusted to the 4-inch mattress on a steel/iron frame, which was difficult, I continued doing the basic things to keep my mind and heart engaged in the things of God. Daily prayer, reading and studying the Word of God, speaking to others about spiritual growth, service, and one's need of Christ. I was glad to start a Bible study. I used the twenty-nine topical lesson study. See Exhibits for the topics.

Each topical study is preceded by a statement of what is believed with associated scriptural passages verifying the position of belief. The answers are given to the questions researched with commentary to root the believer's Christian conviction. I was asked by a student that completed the twenty-nine lessons if I had more studies. I was saddened to let Dennis know that I did not. The same student also suggested I write a book, and at the time I had no interest in doing so. It seemed a boundary I never crossed before, and to be too great of a challenge. I kept that suggestion hidden place in my heart prior to making that decision. I did have the four Gospels questions and answers but without commentary and without those studies being typed.

The individual who suggested I write a book was a land developer and had done well in the real estate market and said he could use the lessons in parochial schools. I was encouraged by his statements and pondered what could be done to accommodate his request. I remember using a few other studies which were done by another church ministry that a person had. I continued using on a one-to-one basis the 29-lesson study and the studies in the Gospels, and the other church resource, which had been given to me to help believers grow in their faith. The interesting thing was that I was not satisfied. When I was at La Tuna, I mentioned Wes having a spiritual inventory guide for believers to discover their spiritual gift. I was able to go through that guide and it confirmed my giftedness. I enjoy breaking down the Word of God to better understand it personally, but also for teaching others to have a greater understanding as well. I love the study of God's word.

As 2012 was preparing to end, I felt moved to do an inductive expository study of the book of Romans. I wanted to research its background, writer, people being written to, and give a verse by verse understanding of the text. I had been asked by my dad if I needed any books, and he would have those sent to me. So, to do any serious study of the New Testament books, I would need tools or resources to aid me. My dad sent me, the Englishman's Greek concordance of the New Testament; an Interlinear Greek-English New Testament; and the Vine's Expository Dictionary of Old and New Testament words. One other individual whose name is Jim, an inmate at Mendota, wanted to participate in ordering some study books to assist my work. He ordered for me Strong's Exhaustive Concordance of the Bible, the New Bible Dictionary - 3rd Edition and Nelson's Complete Book of Bible Maps and Charts. The resources named would be what I needed to dig in and dissect the Word of God with the aid of the Holy Spirit. As God's gift operated in me, I read about the Roman Church at the time the letter was written. I began to structure what should be included in the study. I wanted a purpose statement for studying the letter to the Romans. I wanted a summary of the letter. A table of contents giving the themes of each chapter and the divisions of the book. I wanted to look at every significant word in every verse and identify the Greek term behind the English translation. This was progressive in my thinking not originally targeted. I wanted to provide the Greek meaning for every significant term in the text.

I included a list of associated cross-references to the defined terms so the reader could gain a broader understanding of the use of the word defined. I was led to provide questions derived from each verse. My desire for the Bible students was to assist them in their study, and to reduce their time of research in the tedious work of digging out the truth of God's word. Our Lord is not only interested in His flock of followers knowing the truth of His word, but being morally cleansed by the truth to develop in them His godly characteristic of love, etc. (John 17:17). The combination of both biblical truth and moral cleansing progressively causes effective service by the Holy Spirit. Every believer has a ministry or service to carry out to the glory of God. I desire to fulfill my ministry and desire that you will fulfill yours.

During the time of doing the Roman study, I was invited to join the praise team. I didn't believe I could sing very well, but some of those on the praise team could not sing very well. They were improving, though. I was persuaded to join and have continued while at Mendota. As the days came and went, I continued doing the work in Romans, participating in the church ministry, and elevating my workouts with more push-ups, riding a stationary bike, and using the elliptical to maintain, and or increase my strength and mobility.

Some of the other extracurricular activities occurred around the holidays when tournaments were scheduled. There were table game competitions in Domino's, Spades, Chess, Risk, etc. Outdoor sports included events such as three-on-three basketball, three-point shooting, free throws, bocce, horseshoes, handball, softball, and soccer competitions. Many of the men participated in their regular workout routine, with some working out three times per day. It takes a lot of discipline and commitment to do work outs three times per day. Once a day, over five days, was enough for me at the time. One year, during a spade's tournament, my partner Tennessee and I won the first-place prize. First place typically was given candy like Twix, Snickers, or an Oreo cookies six pack, sometimes even Arizona drinks. I did not participate in the tournaments going forward, due to a lack of interest and greater involvement in church activities, and the study of God's word.

One Christian brother had a marriage workshop study of which a copy was made available to me. I began to inquire if some of the men were interested in the study. There was a respectable number of men who responded wanting to participate. The class was formed, and together we learned how to be better husbands or potential husbands by understanding our wives or women in general and their needs. The workshop relied on the philosophy, approach, techniques, ideas, and concepts presented in two books - "Love and Respect" by Emerson Eggerichs, PH.D. - Nashville, TN: Thomas Nelson, Inc., 2004; and "Staying in Love" by Andy Stanley: Grand Rapids, MI, Zondervan 2010. The workshop had nine sessions of studies scripturally based.

Another area which was a great support to the church at Mendota were volunteer speakers who would come and minister the word of God to our congregation. Some have been coming since I have been at Mendota Camp. Most of the Christian volunteers come on Sundays, during our worship services and deliver a message which was laid on their heart from the word of God. Our chaplain periodically would also speak and does speak when a volunteer is not scheduled or has to cancel for some reason.

Whenever the chaplain is not able to speak when scheduled, and no volunteer is scheduled, I have been asked to speak to the congregation. There are volunteers that also come during Bible study time on Wednesdays at noon. There is an events coordinator who, through the warden, scheduled a Volunteer Appreciation Banquet.

He learned about our praise team and approached our praise team leader and the church leaders at the time, asking for our participation. After the information about the opportunity was presented to those on the praise team, we consented. We were also given the privilege of having two inmates involved, sharing some words of appreciation to the volunteers at the banquet. The church leader and I were both selected to share our appreciation for the whole of the inmates who were recipients of the service of the volunteers. Several of the staff would have words to share, even the warden. We were asked to take no more than a few minutes or so to extend our appreciation. On the day of the occasion, we were asked to arrive at the training center 30 minutes before the volunteers. The camp cooks and kitchen workers prepared the meal for the volunteers. Each one of us were in our inmate uniform and boots issued by the Bureau of prisons. The time came for the event to start with approximately twenty-five volunteers present from various faith backgrounds. After the events coordinator opened the program with the welcome, and our chaplain offered up prayer, the volunteers were able to be served their dinner.

The praise team sang two selections, after which I was up to give what I had prepared and presented to the events coordinator for approval from him and the warden. What I shared with the volunteers can be read in the Exhibits section. The leader of our church did a wonderful job in sharing with the volunteers. He was more spontaneous and had no notes to read from. His name is Oscar. There was applause for our two songs, and both our speeches. This was one of the highlights I experienced while at this camp.

Chapter 19

Moving Through the Years

There was a time at Mendota Camp where the population decreased. More men were being designated to their own region for assorted reasons. Some were going to the drug program called RDAP, where they could have a year reduced from their sentence after completing the course. Others were going to a halfway house and then home. Still others had qualified for the two-point reduction in their sentence and were leaving with months off or on immediate release notification. Therefore, other jobs opened with a shortage of men to fill the job vacancies. You could have two jobs, so I put in for the training center and was cleared to work there as well as a dorm orderly. The training center was out from the camp past the warehouse and maintenance facility, and, it also had some incentives. It was a very nice facility with two offices, a weight room for the officers to work out, conference hall, kitchen, bathrooms, and showers. It was a nice environment. After dividing responsibilities between the orderlies, on occasion you had to lift the dumbbells, and weight bars to clean them or put them back where they belong. There were pull-up bars, ellipticals, and stationary bikes in the best of condition. Occasionally, after an event, there were some food items or bottled water the staff would let go of after cleaning up, by the orderlies. The training center was sort of a get away from the camp due to its seclusion. The staff overseeing it were administrative employees, who were more relaxed than the correctional officers. It was more peaceful as a result. We performed our duties, took our breaks, and returned to the camp dorm area.

While at the camp in Mendota, the program Dateline did a story on my case. There were a few interviews with investors who shared about their loss of investment to our company. The story brought back memories of what had occurred. I remember those who were interviewed, and only wished they could understand our company had no intention of their suffering financial losses. I thought back to the letter I received from the program and did not respond. The program also thought that I had a side to the story, which had not been told.

My appeal, which I lost, argued that the District Court slanted the jury instructions in a way that would favor the government.

Instead of stating that my good faith was a defense that could provide a not guilty verdict from the jury, it only stated that my good faith could be considered. What I represented to the investors was what was represented to me and the other two principals of our company, from the gold agent and mining office. I realize I was negligent in not doing enough due diligence, and not ceasing related to the security demands, but to get ten years plus of time to serve when personally receiving less than 1% of net investment funds received over 3 ½ years, seemed unfair at the time. But it could have turned out worse, after considering many investors suffered and lost great sums of money, property, with one even taking his life. We deeply wished this tragedy never occurred, with the investor taking his own life. Art flew out to offer the wife and family our sincere and heart-felt condolences. Our company paid for the funeral and burial arrangements. While there, it was shared that the investor had some mental illness. Nevertheless, I still feel a sense of being partly responsible for this loss of life. We shared with the pseudo-gold agent the extent to which our investors were going to see the gold transaction close. I came to realize the so-called gold agent had no heart regarding who was being hurt. He only continued his deception to fill his own evil desires. I have accepted the fact that what occurred is irreversible. What is left? I will serve my time unbegrudgingly, and if possible, paying back the investors is my desire. I will be paying restitution for the next 22 years on a quarterly basis while incarcerated, and upon release, monthly as I receive income. I hope the government is dispensing those payments to those who participated in investing in Tri Energy through the court. Fifteen percent (15%) of every cent I make is collected by the U.S. Treasury's litigation department. I understand the percentage can increase based on my revenue. It would be a Godsend if, over time, I could repay the entire debt, which is my prayer.

I am close now to being released to a halfway house, in a year, and will have served nine years at this writing. By the time this book is published I will more than likely be on probation having reached 70 years old or so.

I am grateful to God having preserved me during my prison years, and for the work He has done through me, which I'm in the process of sharing with you.

I want to return to my first inductive expository book study, which was the book or letter to the Romans.

I have earlier named various resources used to do the study. I want to outline more in depth the process that went into the study of Romans and the other books or letters which were also to be completed. The first thing was to pray and ask God to assist me in covering the details needed to give an in-depth systematic study of His word. I had to begin reading the tools I had that would give the background of the Roman epistle (i.e., letter). The information will help me to construct a brief summary of the book, including the purpose of the book, its author, background of the time the book was written, the date of the writing, and something of the message the author was seeking to convey to the readers. The next area was a table of contents with each chapter title or theme and verse divisions. Once these were constructed, after review of resources, things were set for moving into the next area. The third task that needed tackling was that each verse in each chapter needed development of questions coming out of each verse consecutively and in context.

Once I had this accomplished for each chapter, the next area was to take every word or significant word in the verse and writing them out in a vertical fashion. Once the word from each verse was written down from the King James version of the Bible, I had to look up each word in the Strong's Concordance to get the attached numerical digit, which would give the definition of the word in the rear of the concordance. The process was lengthy and laborious. Once the number for the word was identified, I searched the corresponding number for the cross-references, which were the same word used in the same letter or other letters in the New Testament. This would bring consistency of rightly dividing the word. I also used the Vine's Expository Dictionary, which gave comparative definitions of the same Greek word. Sometimes one source had a fuller understanding of how the word was defined.

In the back of Strong's Concordance where the definitions were, was also the Greek terms from which the original language of the New Testament was written, i.e., koine Greek, or the language of the common people in the first century A.D. I wanted each Greek term listed in answers to the questions.

I constructed an answer page for each question or questions presented from each verse.

After the answers for each question were written out, the Greek word(s) before the definitions were given, also following, an insertion of cross-references, if available. Some common words were not defined in the concordances or dictionary of Greek words. In many cases, I provided comments in association with the answer section of each verse and word. On occasion, for clarity, I used some English definitions.
Also included in the book studies are the background research of persons in the text, the city's, the nations, geographical aspects, and conditions of the period. This was either prior to, or current to the writing. Some book studies I have done may have more details of some of these features than others, as the book studies progressively developed having greater detail. The questions for all the book studies were formed out of the New King James Version of the Bible. Please note that some scholars believe the King James Version translation came from inferior, later, Greek manuscripts. I do not concur with this theory. The following is taken from the New King James Study Bible published by Thomas Nelson - noted in the prefix page xiii. I will not reproduce the entire article regarding the New Testament Text, only some of the excerpts as follows:

"The King James New Testament was based on the traditional text of the Greek-speaking churches, first published in 1516, and later called the 'Textus Receptus' or Received Text." Although based on the relatively few available manuscripts, these are representative of many more which existed at the time but only became known later. In the late 19th century, B. Wescott and F. Hort thought that this text had been officially edited by the fourth - century church, but a total lack of historical evidence for this event has forced a revision of the theory.

It is now widely held that the Byzantine Text that largely supports the Textus Receptus has as much right as the Alexandrian or any other tradition to be weighed in determining the text of the New Testament." For those who want to read the entire article, consult the source named earlier.

I'm not against all English translations of the New Testament. Each English translation had a purpose the translators had in mind when they were translated. I personally desire word for word English translation, from the Greek manuscript source I mentioned as a personal study Bible.

There are other good English translation study Bibles such as the New American Standard Bible – NASB, New Revised Standard Version – NRSV, among others. For an easily read English version having common everyday language - the New Living Translation – NLT, and some, like the New International Version – NIV 2011, are acceptable from my perspective. I am partial to the New King James Version Study Bible (1997 edition) because it is based on the Received Text, which is the Greek Text used by Luther, Calvin, and Tyndale among other scholars.

Earlier this year, I took a seminary class in "Principles of Biblical Interpretation." It was a correspondence course in which a proctor, who was the education director of the camp, was appointed. Two members of the church ministry took and finished the course. We both received high marks of 90% or above on the final exam. I mention this because of the books necessary to finish the course, and being tested on the material in the book, had the position on the Alexandrian text as being superior overall. The two authors were not favorable to the King James or New King James translations. Even though the principles learned reinforce the principles already being used, it seems there will be some disagreement on some issues with scholars in the field of textual criticism. The good thing is that you can research both or other positions and decide for yourself which one makes a more credible argument. Those that are Bible students as a sample can compare various passages[6] with the NKJV and the Bible you are using.

---

[6] Matthew 4;4; 17:21; 23:14; Mark 9:29

If the missing part of the passage is in the margin, you have the complete text. If not, you may want a Bible which gives the entire text.

After a six-month process, the inductive expository study of the book of Romans was completed. There would need to be proof reading, editing, and typing. I was fortunate to have a person here at the camp who typed the study of Romans. His name is Sean, one of the church leaders. My neighbor from home, named Joan, did extensive editing on the completion of Romans. Once it was typed, I was able to offer a Bible study class in Romans, which had a very good response. The class lasted over a year. During that time some men were transferred to their region, others went to RDAP, and some went to the half-way house.

When the study came to an end, I had four men still at the camp, who completed the course.

While the study in Romans was being conducted, I felt led to prepare another book study, which was the letter to the Ephesians. I applied the same study process as with the book of Romans. I sensed after finishing the study in Ephesians, I needed to do a study in the letter to the Colossians. I wanted to do all the apostle Paul's prison epistles. Therefore, after finishing the Colossians study, I set my mind to continue the same process of inductive exposition in the letter to the Philippians. After concluding that study, I sought to do the second letter to Timothy, but since there was the first letter to Timothy, I felt I needed to take them in sequence. Once both letters had been finalized, I was driven to prepare the study for Philemon. Since I had started the pastoral letters to Timothy, I felt led to do a study of the letter to Titus, using the same guidelines of inductive expository principles. There was no doubt in my mind that the studies were planted in my heart to do by the power and grace, which comes from the Holy Spirit. Many times, I wondered how I could be engaged in such a work not being a Doctor of Theology, and being in prison? It was by grace. I realized I had the time, and I could use it for the glory of God, and to assist the people of God in their study of the Word of God, which would help them grow and spiritually mature. I thought that many believers could use the studies to grow deeper into the word and save them a lot of time.

I set a goal of doing 20 New Testament books or letters, and one came after the other. It took over four years working many hours daily, and it had to be the Grace of God to sustain the intense effort, or I would have burnt out long before completing the 20th book. The list of books which were drafted can be seen in the Exhibits section.

Once the last letter to the Corinthians was complete, I had no desire to do any more book studies. I indeed needed a break. While doing each inductive study, a talented individual named Corey volunteered to type the book studies. At that time, I had not finished all twenty book studies. Corey was a literary agent, and professional nurse. His typing range was in the 80 to 90 word per minute. Corey was only at the camp for about a year and some months. In that time, he was able to type 14 book studies. The studies exceeded 900 typewritten pages. Since I was in possession of most of the books having been typed, I approached the chaplain regarding holding an inductive expository book study.

The prison is extremely strict about inmates teaching religious classes due to the element of inciting hostility toward other faiths, or belief systems causing radicalization. The chaplain has a master's degree in theology, so he asked me to give him a copy of what would be taught to the students. A copy of the book of Ephesians was made available to him. Upon his review, I was given his consent to conduct the study. The class would take about 4 to 5 months to cover the material in the study. Since the class was lengthy, I asked the chaplain if a certificate could be issued to the participants who finished the course. He consented, and I was elated as well as the men taking the course. It would be the first time this would occur at the camp. When the class commenced the chaplain told me when the class was within two weeks of completion to notify him so he could prepare the certificates. I followed his instructions and alerted him two weeks out from the class concluding and he prepared the certificates. There was good response to the Ephesian class, and the men wanted to do another study. After taking a short break, I informed the chaplain I wanted to have another book study. He asked if he could review the materials for the study. He made a copy of the study and after his review, he gave me the go ahead. I felt twelve men in the study would be the perfect number, so 12 men signed up for the in-depth study of the letter to the Colossians. During the study, a few men left the camp, and a few dropped out.

One of the men who was moving on was the leader of the church ministry.

I had been serving in the ministry, doing the things that had already been stated. The other committed leaders asked me if I would lead church services. I prayed about it and consented. Some of the men who are in leadership were Christian, Bart, and Shawn. The leader who served his time was Oscar. Christian led the praise team. He played the guitar and while at Mendota taught himself to play the piano. Bart was an organizer and kept a record of events held by the church. He also conducted a yearly fast, which was held one month out of the year. The fast was either in February or November. The congregation would select one day to fast 24 hours. Sometimes two separate days would be chosen by a few of the participants. The calendar month with the names filled in would be copied and handed out to those involved. The time was generally from 3 PM to 3 PM.

On the calendar were scriptures, placed to direct the prayers of the men. (References used 7). Sean spoke occasionally and designed the church bulletin. Before my departure from Mendota the positions of leadership were handed to Reniero and AK.

At this time, I want to share some things concerning the Medium security facility. Throughout my stay at the camp, periodically, we would hear ambulance sirens due to disturbances at the Medium. It was discovered that there was a fight or fight involving more than a few, and someone was seriously hurt. Depending on the occurrence, and its seriousness, the Medium would be put on lock down. The lock-down could extend two or three days, and up to a week or more based on the severity of the conflict.

When lock-down occurred, the Medium inmates were restricted to remain in their cells, with no outside movement. Whenever, this happened the inmates from the camp had to go to the Medium to prepare breakfast, lunch, and dinner.

---

[7] 2nd Chronicles 7:14; Isaiah 58; Luke 10:2; Ephesians 6:18-19; 1st Timothy 2:1-5

First, the camp inmates would be asked to volunteer for the morning and lunch shifts. Volunteers were also asked to participate in the evening shift.

Whenever there were not enough volunteers, inmates were randomly assigned to participate during the lock down. The incentive for volunteers was to eat while at the Medium and leave the camp for a brief time. Typically, the grade of food was better than at the camp with greater portions. The reasoning for better quality food in some cases, was to keep the inmates more docile or content, to minimize outbreaks that cause a lockdown.

Also, even though there was a kitchen superintendent and kitchen officers who were experienced food preparers, the experienced inmates would typically prepare the food. Since, over time there were 600-1,200 inmates at the Medium, there were always good food preparers among them. Therefore, the meals were in most cases satisfying to the prison population at large. I can only speak about the Medium across the street, not other Mediums, because I directly experienced the quality of food of this Medium. While at the Low at Safford (900-1,200 inmates), I remember a baker, who made cinnamon rolls once or twice a month on Saturday mornings.

The quality was so good inmates lined up stretching throughout the yard to receive one. The cinnamon rolls were better than most of those sold on the street. Practically all the desserts were great during my stay there. There are a lot of guys in prison with an exceptional amount of talent. The talent is God given and gives value to the individual to use it for good or not. It is the responsibility of the individual to develop their talent. Some of the men surpassed expectation.

The camp volunteers had to leave early in the morning to go through security at the Medium with their ID, and to be checked to prevent bringing anything in unauthorized. The camp crew after passing security was escorted to the kitchen and dining facilities.

The crew had to prepare breakfast, which would typically include, dry cereal, milk, a Danish of some sort or bread, a fruit such as a banana, packets of coffee, packets of sugar/or substitute, eating utensil, Styrofoam cup, and napkins put in a brown bag or Styrofoam or plastic server. All these items had to be organized by each inmate handling a specific area to load the bags in a synchronized fashion.

There had to be a person to count the bags to assure the totals covered all the inmates. All the bags were put into a serving unit with wheels to be rolled out by security officers to each cell unit needing to be served.

Once breakfast was complete, the men took a break and had breakfast. Lunch was more complicated because you had men who had no-flesh diets. Others may have some special diet such as kosher, referred to as common fare. So, peanut butter, tofu, or cottage cheese having the necessary protein content was used to accommodate these groups. Primarily lunch meat for the overall population, like baloney, was served with mayonnaise and mustard packets, potato chips, drink packets, cookie, and fruit. Once this crew completed their task, they had lunch and afterward had to be escorted with officers back to intake with IDs being checked to leave the facility to return to the camp.

Dinner was prepared by another crew from the camp having to go through the security of the Medium as shared earlier. Afterward being escorted like the others by security to the kitchen and dining area. The same types of food for lunch could be served for dinner.

The reason is to deter future outbreaks, to have the men think about their actions before they occur. A hot lunch and dinner meal were served, under ordinary circumstances.

Being put on lockdown is to deliberately make the inmate uncomfortable; to discipline the whole yard as an incentive to hold one's behavior in check, and not upset the tranquil environment of the yard.

The dinner crew, after finishing their task, was able to have dinner.

After which, they cleaned up and were escorted by security back to the intake unit to return to the camp.

While sharing about the Medium, I will communicate another incident, but it occurred at the camp. During the summer, the air conditioning failed. It made our dormitory very difficult to live in, due to the heat. It was hard to sleep and was an unsafe environment, due to germs from the sweat of each inmate. Over a four-day period in this condition, it was finally decided to send the camp to the medium. The camp number was around 67 to 70 individuals. We were told to take only some essentials and that we would be staying on the first floor of one of the housing units. We would be housed at the Medium until the air conditioning could be repaired. The campers were glad to get to an air-conditioned facility. The first-floor unit we arrived at needed cleaning, and that was handled. The sleeping arrangement was not too accommodating, because we would be locked into the cell area every evening and would be let out in the morning. It was something that we had to adjust to. It reminded me of Unit B in Victorville as I waited to be transported to Mendota. The unit had about four TVs elevated in the common area where the inmates congregated after the cells were opened in the morning. We were locked down at a certain time in the evening. There were showers in the unit and an officer's quarters, chairs, a mobile book stand for those who wanted to read and tables for playing cards, dominoes, etc. Once a day we could go to the gymnasium with attached TV room and officer's quarters. There was a basketball court in the gym. In the TV room there were some great murals by artists from the Medium. In the TV area there must have been 7 to 8 TVs and 3 to 4 ping-pong tables. Outside there was a fence enclosure between the gymnasium and a housing unit where one could exercise by walking or running.

When the campers were walking back and forth on the grounds, the Medium inmates had no access to the yard. Some of them waved at some of the campers as a friendly gesture. Once we were back to our housing facility, the exits we used were locked down. The Medium's inmates were let out into the yard by units, not all at once. All our meals were prepared by Medium's kitchen crew. The meals were good.

It finally came time for us to return to the camp after the air conditioning problem was resolved. We were at the Medium for 4 to 5 days. It was good to get back to the camp with the freedom of not being behind such a restricted area.

I had had that experience at Safford, which had more space in the dorm where I resided.

Chapter 20

The City of Light

Early in the ministry at Mendota, one of the brothers asked me if money wasn't an issue what would I do? The believer's name was Joe. I told him I would develop a City of Light. Joe had an architectural background, among other skills. Joe and I began to sit together and put my thoughts and concepts on paper. I would visualize what the facilities would be used for and the interior layout. He would sketch the building facilities. As I prepared to lay out my ideas, keep in mind this is a hypothetical concept if money were no issue. The name City of Light is taken from the passage in Matthew 5:14 where Jesus refers to his followers as the light of the world. A city that is set on a hill that cannot be hidden. In verse sixteen it states, "Let your light so shine before men, that they may see your good works and glorify your Father in heaven." The believer is to be a light to the world. What does light do? It gives sight. If it is a light house, it steers one away from the danger of collision with land or hidden rocks. The intent is to preserve life. Light also gives direction. It makes things visible, like the headlights of an automobile at night. The headlights assist you in navigating to where you want to go, i.e., your destination. The intent of the City of Light is to preserve life and steer people to a relationship with God through loving service to them by good works. After prayer, the first step is to secure a substantial amount of land – 1,000 acres to start, in a commercial zone area. The first building on the property would be a church sanctuary with a seating capacity of 1,500 in the auditorium. The following would occupy the interior all-inclusive and not limited only to what is named.

* Pastor's office/study/restroom/ shower
* Assistant Pastor office
* Christian Education Dir. Office
* Church secretary office
* Baptismal/pool
* Conference room
* Fellowship Hall
* Sound room/multimedia
* Prayer/room
* 10/classrooms
* Bible/bookstore
* Choir/loft

- * Workstation
- * Kitchen
- * Men & women's restrooms
- * Maintenance storage garage
- * Nursery
- * Two choir dressing rooms
- * Auditorium/seating
- * Utility room

The appropriate parking spaces would be provided for the worshiping attendees. The City of Light will want to attract a core group of Christ centered believers, understanding that we are His workmanship created in Christ Jesus for good works.[8] God has also given the church through Christ, gifted leaders to prepare, train, and spiritually mature believers, in order for them to do the work of ministry or service. The process comes by speaking the truth of the Word of God, through a loving obedient demeanor to the word.[9] I found in obeying the word of God it brings joy to my heart. When I want to please God, I first spend time with him in prayer, then the reading, and study of His word. I found this to be very important, because of the peace and comfort it brings with insights. My deepest longing is to be used by God. I also want to influence other peoples lives for the Kingdom. Even though I have stumbled, I can still choose to follow what is of worth; what is of eternal value. My aim is to be a vessel of honor. The last chapter in my life I want to be strong for the service of God. God has developed in me what matters, which is an eternal perspective. In general, it is never too late for anyone on this side of life. It is about making the right choices. When I grasped the vision of my role in going through an ongoing process of maturity, with the realization I could participate in the service of good works to help others to come to know Christ and grow spiritually, this was exciting to me. I have realized every Christian has vulnerabilities and needs an understanding brother or sister to come along side to provide support. We are to bear each other's burdens.

There are no perfect, sinless Christians. Some take longer to work through their weaknesses or issues than others. I have learned if anyone is without sin, let that person cast the first stone. As a balance, I know I need to be held accountable, not so much a misstep here or there, although I need to acknowledge it, but for ongoing disregard for observing the word of God.[10] This is scary for me.

---

[8] Ephesians 2:10 ; [10] 1st Timothy 5:19-20,22,24-25; 1st Corinthians 5:9-13; Ephesians 4:32; 1st John 1:9
[9] Ephesians 4;11,12,15

These are some principles on which I stand, by the direction of the Holy Spirit and the word of God, with others who will labor to establish a congregation of Christ-centered disciples. In regard to specific areas of good works, these are not good works to earn my way to Heaven, but good works produced because I have been born again by repentance and faith in Jesus Christ.[11] Therefore, if one wants to work the work of God, he or she needs to take the first step. This is what I did, believing in Jesus Christ whom God sent.[12] Otherwise, all my so-called good works would be of no value to gain admittance to Heaven without knowing the Lord Jesus Christ. I have come to understand that the primary good work that has affected my drive is to share the good news of Jesus Christ, make disciples, and love people. What gives me deep conviction is to know that Jesus rose from the dead and made bodily appearances to his disciples over a 40-day period.[13] He ascended into heaven.[14] My expectation is that one day I will ascend into Heaven. As the bible says for Christians, "To be absent from the body is to be present with the Lord."[15] What brings joy to my heart is that one day I'll be called home and leave this aging body, with its deteriorating condition, to receive a new eternal glorified body like the body Christ rose in.[16] I have found that the sharing of the good news by the power of the Holy Spirit, brings individuals into a true relationship with God. Everyone needs to know that God loves them so much that He sent His Sinless Son from Heaven, into the world to be our sin bearer, (i.e., to be our substitutionary sacrifice before God to pay the penalty we deserve for our sins by His suffering and death). The innocent for the guilty. The purpose for His death is so humanity would escape personal judgment in the flames and torments of Hell originally created for the devil and his fallen angels. God has to judge and punish sin, or He would not be just. Jesus is our Deliverer, Hero, and Rescuer. I have felt the heat over my stove when making oatmeal or rice when stirring it into boiling water. I could feel the heat. I had to remove my hand because it was so hot. I could not imagine what my whole body would feel like engulfed in that kind of heat. The love for sin, from my standpoint, is not worth the temporal pleasure of sin for me. Just knowing the payment of sin is eternal separation from God and Heaven, is not something I want to experience after the horrific punishment Christ

---

[11] John 3:3; Ephesians 2:8,9; Romans 6:23
[12] John 6:28,29
[13] Acts 1:3
[14] Luke 24:50,51; Acts 1:9-11
[15] 2nd Corinthians 5:8
[16] Philippians 3:20-21

went through to purchase me. After all the years of studying the Word of God, I have complete confidence in knowing I have eternal life through Jesus Christ once this life ends.

In continuing the hypothetical, if money were no issue as this question was presented to me by Joe, certain funds would be allocated to establish a benevolence fund to assist the needs of those who are struggling for one reason or the other, who are part of the congregation in the City of Light. Scripture verifies the need to support the weak.[17] The word weak means to be feeble (in any sense), diseased, lacking physical strength, especially as a result of age or illness, and being unable to work.

A Spirit-led core focus group, having the gifts of mercy would convene to understand the needs in this area and address the issues, and provide services in each case. The elderly widows would come under this umbrella who have no family to help care for their monthly needs. Financial assistance is just one aspect. More than likely, the senior sisters and brothers in the faith would need some friendships and visits.[18]

The planning of a senior's home would occur forming a core focus group which is gifted in the planning and building trades. The plan would be developed to accommodate a 100 live-in-unit facility. The necessary acreage of land would be allocated on the 1000-acre property. The planning of the hospital in the City of Light would be another phase of the services provided to handle the needs of those who are sick among us. A gifted core focus group of health professionals would convene to develop a strategy, or approach, which would provide services of a 100-bed facility. The feasibility study and budget would be developed for the facility and internal equipping of the hospital. A portion of the 1,000-acre property would be allocated. The next area of concern is for orphans, abandoned children, and babies. A gifted and specialized core focus group would be assembled to develop a plan of approach to address the needs and concerns of these groups, and the extent of the services which would be provided.

---

[17] Acts 20:34,35
[18] James 1:27

The facility costs, staffing, and equipment acquisition, etc. would be presented in a comprehensive plan. A portion of the 1,000-acre property would be allocated to howse and to minister in these areas.

Another concern to be addressed is the establishment of the Christian education ministry. Two departments would be established:

The first would address the equipping of the congregation through home Bible study groups and on-site church classes utilizing curriculum to build up the body. 2. Establish a private school for K through 12th grade, integrating core learning and academic areas of reading, writing, and math with Christian doctrine and values. The school would be a combination of the students receiving a Christian education, but also testing and evaluation for business and vocational training. The aspect of physical fitness will be included as a part of the curriculum. A gifted core focus group specializing in the educational arena would convene to establish these two departments. The preschool development area would also be considered. A portion of the 1,000-acre property would be allocated for these ministries.

Our ministry in the City of Light would seek to encourage the believing body, to employ their gift both spiritually and naturally to build up fellowship and reach out to the community. Many lives are broken and in need of the lifesaving message of the gospel. The Lord Jesus mentions some areas that qualify as good works in Matthew 25:35-36. It states, "For I was hungry, and you gave me food; I was thirsty, and you gave me drink; I was a stranger, and you took me in; I was naked, and you clothed me; I was sick, and you visited me; I was in prison, and you came to me."

Some of these must be approached with caution, due to the state of man's fallen condition considering these perilous times. We would be wise, and prayerful. The ministries I propose would seek to be sure we are being led by the Holy Spirit in these matters.

Another part of the vision the City of Light would have is a sports and recreation complex, which would include the following:

1. A multipurpose gymnasium, with adjacent exercising classrooms.
2. A two-screen two-section movie theater with concessions counter.
3. A 15-Lane bowling alley, game room and food bar.
4. An Olympic sized swimming pool with diving boards of various meters, with men and women dressing rooms.
5. A sports field for football, soccer, baseball, track and field events.
6. A number of tennis courts. The assembling of believers, having experience in these areas, would be brought together to plan out each phase of the building project to be undertaken.

Also, I would consider a few food franchises to border the property which would be owned by the City of Light. The scripture, mentioned in Matthew 25, addresses an area that I would want to see ministry occur. That area is reaching the incarcerated. Since I have been incarcerated, each prison facility I was in had ministers of the gospel, who shared the Word of God, either on a Sunday or during the week by conducting a Bible study. The reaching out to men, women, and youth incarcerated is a good work, in which the City of Light would participate. Through prayer and fellowship with those in prison facilities and upon release, a release-program would be established providing temporary housing for qualified ex-offenders who are Christians or became Christians while behind the walls. Certain criteria would have to be met to be admitted. A core focus group will be set up to establish guidelines for one to enter the home in the City of Light. The intent of the home is to provide not only an address for the released individual, and the necessity of continued spiritual growth, but assistance in becoming employed. The core focus group would set a standard of godly character in Christian service while in prison, which would be a determining guideline for applicants. A core group would provide the other needed standards as well. Once one qualifies for admittance into the released program, there would be aptitude testing and occupational personality evaluation to determine what areas would be suitable in preparation to pursue an occupation. Once a profile for individuals is established, that individual can be shown how to pursue a life profession or programs. The homes would be built in stages.

The four homes to be built would have in each - four bedrooms, four bathrooms, a large kitchen, two family rooms, a large dining room, indoor washers and dryer, a large living room, and 4 car garages.

Two of the homes would be for young men 15 to 17 years of age, and the other for adult men 18 years of age and older. The other two homes would be for young girls ages 15 to 17, and the other for women 18 years of age and older.

The foregoing are some thoughts of mine for consideration for the City of Light if there were no limitation of funds. I will share some added thoughts as I close this section regarding the City of Light.

I would seek to build a conference center and motor lodge to accommodate associated events centered around conferences, and sporting events. Our entertainment and sports complex should attract family-oriented organizations and associations.

The City of Light would be a gated community, like the entrance into a gated residential community or an amusement park, or a very large multifaceted gated estate. It would have its own security team. Each aspect and service of the City of Light will be self-sustained. Each aspect and design would need five-year plans.

Since God is the great architect of the universe with the capacity to make billions of galaxies, having called every star by name, He can give the wisdom for bringing together all the resources needed for the City of Light, if it is a project approved by His will.

I do not believe this is too big for God. There would be openness for adjustments or modifications. Things would be built in phases. The thoughts expressed come from a limited examination of biblical good works, which would cause men to glorify the eternal God and Father of our Lord Jesus Christ.

Chapter 21

The Straight Talk Program

I want to share with my readers about a noteworthy program, which was made available to the inmates at Mendota Camp. One of the staff psychologists, in conjunction with our Camp Administrator, launched a Straight Talk Program. This was different from the Scared Straight Program that has been televised for years. The staff psychologist designed a program for inmates to speak about the experiences that put us in prison. It is a non-threatening approach, which gives the inmate an opportunity to share his story with the hopes of deterring an at-risk youth from heading down the path that could bring incarceration or even death. The staff psychologist and Administrator contacted middle schools and high schools in our area and received a favorable response. A camp electronic bulletin, as well as a flyer, were both posted to attract those inmates who were interested in participating. At first, I thought I was too busy with my other commitments to get involved. One inmate approached me and asked if I was going to interview and share my story with the youth. His prodding caused me to decide to give it a try, because my story may influence a youth to turn from taking the wrong path and instead pursue the right path. As a group of approximately 10 to 12 inmates responded, we were given a briefing on the program and had to be ready to share what we would say to the youth when we met later. As the group came together the second time, we were placed in pairs. Only the Staff Psychologist and Camp Administrator heard the group, as we were paired off. The rest of the participants had to stand or sit outside in the hallway. The auditions were held in a multipurpose room. As each pair made their presentations before the coordinators, each pair was given suggestions on what could be said or not be said. Constructive notes were taken during each presentation. The following week we would meet to see what progress was made. The person I was paired with met every day to practice, until our group rehearsal. I wrote out my speech and committed it to memory. The Camp Administrator said my speech in the beginning, when it was read verbatim, was too preachy towards the end. So, I had to alter my talk towards the end. Everyone needed to give a three-minute talk.

Everyone, as we met in a group to give our talks, had to adjust. There were eight finalists. Some of the men wanted to ad lib their speech, or shoot from the hip, but the coordinators wanted the speech to be consistent, with no new elements of surprise, because of the possibility of something being said that was inappropriate. Everyone needed to memorize their three-minute talk. Every week we practiced our speech before the coordinators to refine and polish our presentations. There would be four men that would present their talks to the students. The men were selected on the content of their story, the way they presented it, and how relative they were to the youth. I started in a group of four to present, but in one of my presentations stumbled in presenting. I was put in the secondary group of four, which would be alternates for anyone who stumbled in their presentation. All the speeches centered around how each inmate wound up in prison, what impact it had on loved ones, and why one would not want to make the mistake or mistakes made by the inmate. The at-risk youth could be troubled, physically abused, involved in drug use, teen pregnancy, gang affiliation, from a broken home, having no motivation to acquire a basic education, or truancy.

The eight men rehearsed daily until we had our first meeting with the youth and their accompanying staff. The day before our meeting the visitor's room needed to be arranged and cleaned. The need for tables from the classrooms was brought in with classroom chairs for the staff and students. The refreshment tables needed covering. Tableware included small plates, napkins, and glasses. The coordinators provided cookies, and ice water for the guests. The eight of us sat in two rows, four in each row, facing the guests. The Staff Psychologist opened the event with a welcome and short speech with statistical data centering around at-risk youth. After his presentation, the Staff Psychologist asked the four presenters to stand in front of the guests in a horizontal row. The first speaker shared his story and each of the four men gave their presentations consecutively. All did an outstanding job. Each in sequence, after his talk introduced the next speaker. Once the last speaker spoke, he informed the guests that we would come and sit with them, a few men at each of the four tables where the youth were seated.

After 15 minutes of interaction with the youth asking questions with the school staff, we rotated to the next table for another 15 minutes.

The process of connecting with the youth, answering questions, and engaging them in conversation lasted for an hour. Refreshments were made available after the hour of interaction, at which point there was freedom to move around and talk freely with the youth or staff members from their school. A Straight Talk brochure was given to all of those who visited the event.

The warden of our institution stopped in before the men presented. After about 15 minutes of open interaction, everyone was called to be seated in their respective seats, as the event was preparing for closure. One staff member from the school made comments on the event giving compliments to the speakers and the interaction seen. Also, one of the leaders of the group of students who came expressed how the meeting and interaction made a difference in how he would view life from that day forward. All the students felt the same way, leading to an applause of gratitude for having them come. The meeting ended with the Staff Psychologist closing out the meeting.

The unfortunate thing about the event held for the Straight Talk program was that it would be the first and last. This was due to the Bureau of Prisons Regional Office Director shutting down the program, because of some policies that were never made clear to us. Since I memorized my presentation, I want to make it available. My talk may help someone to reconsider making wrong decisions that can bring sorrow and regret. It can steal years from one's life and family. My speech can be reviewed in the Exhibits section.

Based on our outreach to the youth, I want to share some research regarding at-risk youth and youth overall in the U.S. as follows.

- There are 42 million youth between the ages of 10 to 19, who make up 12.9% of the population. U.S. Department of Health and Human Services (HHS)
- In 2017 almost 1 in 6 adolescents - 16% were living in families with income below the federal poverty guidelines. (HHS)

- 1 in 6 adolescents are more likely to suffer from behavioral or emotional problems and engage in unhealthy behaviors – such as eating unhealthy diets, physical inactivity, smoking, early initiation of sexual activity. Taken from HHS - Office of Population Affairs.
- In 2007, nearly 40% of children in the U.S. lived in low-income families with incomes at or below 200% of the federal poverty level. HHS Office of Assistant Secretary for Planning & Evaluation (ASPE)
- 1 in 9 individuals between 16 to 24 are neither working nor attending school. Taken from Wallet Hub (WH)
- 70% of young adults today are ineligible to join the US military because they failed academic, moral, or health qualifications.

Research shows that when one grows up in environments with economic problems and lack of role models, they are more at risk for poverty, early pregnancy, and violence, especially in adulthood. (WH) Children from low-income families are more likely to:

- have sex before age 16
- become a gang member
- attack someone or get into a fight
- steal something worth more than $50
- run away

Some additional reasons for at-risk youth being vulnerable:

- lack of family support – low parent educational level; family economic hardship; single parent family
- lack of professional opportunities
- ineffective school disciplinary measures

The positive outcomes to youth empowerment programs are improved social skills, improved behavior, increased academic achievement, increased self-esteem, and increased self-efficacy - (Social Solutions).

There are faith-based programs to assist at-risk youth in building character and offering an assortment of life skills to assist youth in finding their niche in a challenging world.

Chapter 22

The Downside and Upside

I want to share some of the sad things that occurred in prison from my experience, along with some positives. One of the biggest injustices is being punished for the actions of others. There are those who bring into the compound contraband. This can range from tobacco, marijuana, other drugs, alcohol, cell phones, muscle enhancing powders, clothing, tennis shoes, weapons, etc. This is all common knowledge throughout the prison system. When there is a shakedown, which is a massive search by the correctional officers called by the warden, all inmates must leave the dorm facility. Each is patted down, shoes taken off, and on occasion, strip-searched. Strip-searched is the most humiliating experience in prison from my view. Strip-searched means you strip down, butt naked. You must lift your private parts in front for a check for any contraband. Then you must turn around bend over and spread your buttocks because people hide things in that area. When one is taken through this experience, when you know you are not at fault, you feel a sense of disgust and physical violation. One of the inmate prison codes is you do not snitch on a fellow inmate. If one does, you can be set up with contraband put in your locker or thrown into your bunk area when a shakedown occurs. Also, you can be labeled as a snitch and ostracized by the general group you affiliate with. It is rare, but you may even be attacked by a group of men if you're found to be a snitch.

Another penalty for the finding of contraband in the camp is to have certain privileges taken from the general population, when again, you have not violated that rule. Our camp was penalized by removing the majority of our regular commissary items from the commissary list, and as a result, limiting what could be bought. The whole camp was put on a SHU (Special Housing Unit) commissary list. The restriction is typically one meat item per week, no beans or rice, one candy item, no peanut butter, a cookie item, or potato chip item, but you could not have both. When the commissary items are limited, one can lose weight because the portions in the dining hall are not always filling or palatable. Most of the hygiene items are available with the SHU commissary list.

This restriction went on for months at our camp. The last thing that occurs in conjunction with the SHU commissary list due to violation of rules is contraband being found anonymously.

The administrator can put a restriction on our recall time. The typical time when the camp needs to return to the dorm can be as late as 8:45 PM. As I am writing, our time to return to the dorm is 6:00 PM. Anonymous contraband limits outdoor recreation or outside leisure time. These restrictions are placed on the entire population, even though the majority are being punished for the few violators. The 6 PM restriction has been in place for approximately 120 days due to the contraband discovery, and rediscovery. Contraband being found anonymously can also remove T.V. privileges. The frustration seems to never end. The way through it all is to stay occupied with the routine you have, which for me is ministry and some physical exercise. There is also your radio combination with your MP3 player. I have my Bible, music, ministry, prayer, and news programs which help. The opportunity to study the word of God has been not only enlightening but settling in these times of trying circumstances. The fellowship with the brothers in Christ is comforting and energizing. Time continues no matter what is taking place, which means one is coming closer and closer to going home. I had a team meeting with my case manager a week ago. The meeting typically is for updating one's programming activity, which is required by the Bureau of prisons, to make sure the inmate is preparing himself for eventual release and integration back into society successfully. Since I am nearing my halfway house date to return to the area where I live, it was particularly an important meeting for me. In my last team meeting, my case manager said he would put me in for a year due to the amount of time I had served incarcerated and having no custody violations.

Also, I had a good record of programming in institutions from the beginning until now. I had been hearing that there were governmental cutbacks and reducing of halfway houses across the nation, which meant limited bed space in the halfway houses. All of this was made clear in my meeting with my case manager in October 2017.

He said he would not be able to provide a year's combination of six months' halfway house and six months home confinement to finish my prison term. Rather, he could only put me in for six months, which reduced my expectation of getting back to my home region by six months.

My early expectation that was communicated to family and friends, was my return to my home region in the summer of 2018. It now had to be revised to me getting to my home area in December 2018. This was a disappointment for me, and for my family and friends. However, everything works together for good to those who love the Lord, to those who are called according to His purpose. So, there is a purpose for the additional six months here in Mendota if nothing changes. I'm not to worry about anything, but in prayer and petition make my request known to God, and the peace of God which passes all understanding will guard my heart and mind in Christ Jesus (an ad lib version).[19] I am very thankful to God for keeping and supplying the needs of my family, while keeping me safe during this prison experience. I have taken a victim impact class while here, during the early part of this year. Whenever a crime is committed it does not just affect the immediate family, but a whole host of others.

In my case, hundreds upon hundreds have been affected. I could never repair the hurt and loss to all the people involved in investing in my company. I could never, in my power, restore all the losses incurred, but what I can do is never travel down that road again. If I had the means to repay the investors at least their principal amounts, I would. There is not a week that goes by where I have not thought about what happened. All who suffered losses are victims. I will have lost 10+ years of my life for my part in the loss to the investors. My family has suffered losses which can never be repaid to them. Those years are gone. All that can be done is to hopefully repair the relationships, which were shattered. All must be approached by taking one step at a time, and with God's help, healing can occur. Love covers a multitude of sin, and love never fails. Loving actions will be the foundation, in Christ, to repair those relationships. May love prevail...

---

[19] Romans 8:28; Philippians 4:6

I want to say again, I am so, soooo sorry to all who have been hurt and suffered financially, physically, and emotionally. I ask each of you to please forgive me.

Since Mendota is a relatively new facility, open for little more than six years at the time of this writing, the programs are limited. There has been a non-profit class that has been taught, which covers the 501 C3 status. The class was taught by one of the church leaders, Sean.

Sean had worked in several non-profit organizations accumulating 20 years or more in experience. The class covered the corporate structure, grant writing, along with fundraising ideas with forms to apply, etc. Sean taught another class called Personal Skills Management. The class was one of self-discovery, promoting what each person is to become in character, the study of the nature of morals and of moral choices, handling our strengths and weaknesses, finding what profession or vocation our personality is well suited for, using the Myers Briggs inventory test. I was amazed how accurate the test was, regarding my personality's suitable vocations.

Another worthwhile class was how to start a small business, which was taught by another co-inmate named Frank. Frank owned his own business, which was very profitable, but his partner made some bad decisions that were not disclosed to Frank. These caused him to lose his business and end up incarcerated. Frank's class covered a business plan, for a startup business. Some topics were reducing risk by buying an existing business or franchise, benefits, and drawbacks, writing the right plan for your business idea, calculating customer, market, and sales opportunities, analyzing and using the experience of your competition, creating sales, using social media as a powerful marketing and sales tool, operations process, estimating your start up financial requirements, and other areas.

Earlier this year, a Serve Safe class was made available for the camp by the education department, which dealt with handling food in the food service industry.

Anyone working in restaurants, supermarkets, fast food, and other establishments, must have food handlers who went through training on how to handle food safely. We also learned there must be a food-service certified manager in each establishment.

One other program made available to the camp was training to drive a forklift. It was an owner-subcontractor who trains aspiring forklift operators, and when the training is completed, provides a certification card which can assist in obtaining a job in that area. Many men at Camp took this class, which is a combination of classroom instruction and practice on a forklift. The federal prison system attempts to provide various classes by which the inmate can learn skills that can assist in acquiring work upon release.

One of the ongoing requests from prison inmates is viable vocational opportunities, to learn to find work when going home.

Many of the prison facilities offer commercial driver training from the standpoint of a training manual, but have no practical experience available, which is a flaw in the program. I heard there are a few federal prison sites in the nation providing practical commercial driver training.

The institution here is making available community college courses for the inmate to take for college credit. There is a library of community college correspondence courses accessible to the men. The classes increase their knowledge in various subjects, but many do not avail themselves of the resources for various reasons. Others, however, do access the studies which I observed firsthand.

A few other classes held by several of the men involved learning how to trade on the stock market. I mentioned while at La Tuna camp, my bunkie was a trader and had done well in the profession. He had a class, but after a few sessions it seemed complicated to me, so I stopped attending. Two of my Christian friends were learned in this area, so I decided to take another look. One of them, Christian, studied for five years while at Mendota, the theory, strategies, and discipline of trading. I gained a better overall understanding of trading through his class.

One statistic stood out, 90% of beginning traders lose money, fail, and quit the first year. Also, Reniero was a general securities representative, authorized to sell a large array of securities such as stocks, bonds, options, mutual funds, etc. He was successful in this line of work. One other individual, by the name of Scott, had the same securities classification as Reniero. Scott also did well. I spent a great deal of time with these two men, looking at trading in the Forex currency market. I participated in charting, and strategies for buying and selling various currencies. It is interesting to note that Jesus spoke about money and trading.[20] Reniero had a partner that caused his incarceration. He was still fighting his case at this writing.

Some of the men have degrees and will return to the workplace in their skills. Some will have to change their trade or vocation, due to the connection of their trade with their offense.

Another positive occurrence at the camp that started out as a negative, is the following. We had an inmate that had nightmares, during the time the camp was asleep overall. The individual would wake up screaming, and this went on numerous times over a few weeks. There were those who became very annoyed at this occurrence, to the extent of making threats. It was suggested that we should come together as brothers in Christ and pray over this individual, seeking God to remove what was occurring in the mind of this individual late at night. We asked the inmate if he would allow us to pray for him, and he consented. A time was set for us to come together and pray for this person who was tormented. When we got together, three or four brothers prayed for the deliverance of the inmate. God showed up and worked a miracle, and our doctor friend from that moment forward had no more disturbing nightmares at the camp. He was led to Christ days after and began to attend church services.

Another of the unfortunate occurrences at the camp, which should not occur involving men, are verbal conflicts which lead to physical altercations. I had some verbal conflicts, but they did not come to fist-fighting.

---

[20] Luke 19:11-27

In one instance, there was a dispute over working out in an exercise room, where one race did not want the other race to be in the room at the same time. In higher security levels this type of mindset occurs. But when one has worked their way down from the higher level to a camp, there should be a change in one's mindset. What has been ingrained should be let go because you are making preparations to go home. On this occasion no one let anything go, so the offended inmate got a person to make sure he was not double teamed. So, one on one, they fought with no interruption. Then the offended inmate fought with the second person. It appeared that, this should have been the end of the conflict. It was not the end. The offended inmate continued to fight with the primary instigator over a three-day period in the dorm.

Finally, the authorities found out about what was occurring. The whole dorm was called to line up by their lockers and had to take off their shirts and stretch out their arms and hands to determine if they engaged in the fighting.

Both men were removed from the dorm and were escorted to the Medium to the SHU. The campers were always kept separate from those in the SHU who were from the Medium. Over time (say 90 days) one of the inmates shipped out, and the other returned to the camp. Many of the camp inmates were stunned over this incident and did not sleep well over the three-day skirmish. Most of these men had only experienced a camp, and no higher-level security. Many were on edge.

A year or more had passed, and on another occasion two men of opposite race who knew each other from another location had a disagreement. I do not remember what exactly happened, but it all occurred in the barbershop regarding the use of clippers. Well, that evening, I am in the restroom preparing to leave, and these two men are fighting having worked their way into the restroom. A throng of people were viewing the altercation. I, and another inmate, attempted to hold people back and eventually the two stopped fighting. I, and another person, began to tell everyone that it was over. I go back to my bunk area to settle in, being well into the evening, and I see a group of men walking toward the TV room. I knew that this fight had not ended.

I walked over two aisles from my bunk and saw the two men talking back and forth, and suddenly the fight started all over again, but this time with greater numbers. This time I knew I could not break up the fight. I went back to my bunk to wait to see if things would settle down.

The next thing I knew was the door leaving the dorm was pushed open sounding off the alarm alerting the officer on duty that someone had left the dorm or messed with the door. Everyone involved in the fight immediately stopped, putting things back in order like chairs that were used as a weapon, trash containers, and tables that were out of place due to the scuffle. Everyone either went back to their bunk or went into the TV room. The officer had no clue what had happened. He walked around checking the dorm. All seemed calm. Once the officer left, the mediators came together to call a truce and end the conflict. Had the person not pushed the door, things in the dorm would have become worse. Someone would have really been hurt seriously. The conflict started with two, then a group, and thank God it did not spill over to the whole dorm. Some of the inmates who were not involved were still on edge until midnight. These things should not happen at a camp. The authorities found out about the disturbance and some of the men ended up going to the SHU. There are informants in the camp.

I later found out the next day that another Hispanic group wanted to enter the fight but was held back by the shot caller who told them it was not their fight. This group was called the Pisa's, who are Hispanic foreigners not born in America. There are different gangs or groups that make up the Hispanics. The Sureños (Southerners), and Norteños (Northerners), among others. Just as among blacks there are the Bloods and the Crips, etc. It is unfortunate that these groups are divided when our Creator made each and every one of us to dwell together peaceably. We each have value in God's sight, given gifts and talents for good use, not evil. The first principle to be a wise individual comes from Proverbs. In the first chapter it states, "The fear of the Lord is the beginning of knowledge, but fools despise wisdom and instruction." Later in chapter 1, it discourages being a part of a gang (even though the Bible does not use that term), because of the consequences of not taking heed to wisdom. Respect should be given to God first and foremost. He is Lord over the physical and the spiritual realms.

The term fear means reverential awe and respect which is given to our Maker, who will be our final Judge. We are to love our neighbor as we love ourselves. Matthew 22:39. We are all brothers, humanly speaking, no matter what color, and created by God. Walking in the Creator's principles will steer one away from decisions which will destroy our lives. Bad decisions can land one in prison. Every person tempted to do evil should read at least the first 10 chapters of Proverbs in the Bible. Those verses can help to preserve our life in part if we're willing to listen.

As I continue to stay focused on assisting men grow in their faith in the camp, aside from personal study, occasionally on Wednesdays at noon, there is a Bible study that I mentioned earlier in this book. Whenever a volunteer, or the chaplain, is not able to come in, I have been asked to lead the study. I wanted to take the men through a New Testament book or letter called the First Letter to the Thessalonians. The book was written to new Christian believers who lived in Greece. Timothy, a co-laborer with the apostle Paul, brought back a report having helped to establish the believing community in Thessalonica. The Thessalonian church was a church on the move for our Lord and Savior. This church was commended by Paul, after he and his missionary team had spent three Sabbaths sharing the good news of the peace God was bringing to those who were receptive to the message. The letter also speaks of the quality of ministry presented to these people, and the godly character exhibited. Paul encourages the believers to grow and live for Christ, under persecution, which was being experienced because of their newfound beliefs.

These new believers were coming out of pagan idolatry. The last few chapters, deal with purifying our lives by avoiding sexual immorality, and with those who had died as believers. The future events of the coming of the Lord Jesus, in the clouds, to remove believers from the Earth, and the day of the Lord which brings judgment on the Earth are described. I was motivated by the great insights outlined in the first letter to the Thessalonians.

The unfortunate predicament was that this was one of the five remaining letters to be typed. I was determined to go on with the study by asking the questions in the lessons, and having the men answer from the verses from which the questions were derived. After the men gave their answers, I would then go to the answers and study notes for greater clarity and answer verification. During the second week I had a participant, whose name was Nick, wanting to type the lessons. I consented with joy and realized God had placed Nick in the study. Anyone who typed had a challenge, due to the typewriters the Bureau of prisons purchased. The typewriters were designed to type legal documents. I expressed to Nick the difficulty he would have in typing the book. He did not waiver, and over a period of time completed the entire document. My humble thanks and appreciation to Nick....

At Mendota Camp, there are no computers available to do general typing tasks. The computers we have are used for emails, and for purchasing music for the MP3 players bought from the commissary. There are computers used for GED (General Education Development), but only when testing is occurring. Many of the men have requested classes in the use of computers and the software packages, which are needed to head down the road of becoming computer literate. Some prison facilities have computer classes to learn the basics, but to date Mendota camp has not made those classes available. I am hoping that will change.

The last area to mention on the downside of the camp, is the confiscation by the correctional officers of the accumulation of items for the gift bags given to new inmates coming to Mendota camp.

Some officers were aware of what the items were for. Other officers were not. Some were under the impression the items were being sold or used in gambling. The unfamiliar officer, during his search of lockers, when coming across the laundry bag with all the items to give freely to the new inmate, would take the bag. The value could range from around $50 to $100. It would cause the Christians and others who donated to have to start all over. If a new inmate arrived it was difficult to assist him, although we pulled together to help him. This was a good effort to help someone in need.

On several occasions, we lost our laundry bag full of items. We developed another strategy to take care of the issue.

I want to express a hearty hello to all the brothers across the prison system I had the privilege to meet and interact with. I know most of you are at home. Peace to each of you in Jesus' name!

Chapter 23

God at Work - What About the Great Commission?

Earlier this year, i.e., 2017, during the Easter celebration weekend, God was at work in our fellowship. In typical fashion during the Good Friday service, our chaplain spoke. Every religious group has a holy day in the year where a special meal is served, granted by the Bureau of Prisons. There was also a volunteer that came and joined the service as a guest and ate with us after the service. The praise team led in worship, and communion was administered by the chaplain in remembrance of our sins, which our Lord paid for with His body and blood. Due to other obligations the volunteers and chaplain have on Easter Sunday, I like calling it Resurrection Sunday, they could not attend. So, the inmates' service on Sunday was just with inmates. The Resurrection Sunday service would have three men share what was on their hearts after the opening prayer and worship in songs. Each person sharing would take from 5 to 6 minutes to deliver the message impressed upon them by God. God worked in the midst to direct the giving of an invitation, where three men raised their hands to invite Jesus Christ into their lives through the prayer of repentance, and trust in our Savior's finished work on the cross. Feeling responsible for these men who were new in the faith, over the next week I engaged each one to participate in lessons, which would advance their spiritual growth.

During that time, the Lord started laying on my heart to reach out to a few other men, who consented to sit down with me to walk them through the plan of salvation. When the time came to meet with each one, they each responded to the good news of what Jesus Christ had done for them in taking the punishment each of us deserves. I had learned that everyone who comes to Christ by grace (unmerited favor, unearned favor), through faith, receives as a deposit in their heart or life - the righteousness of Christ, (i.e., perfect moral standing before God) as a free gift.[21] This is the requirement to enter Heaven upon death.

---

[21] Romans 5:17-19

Everyone who comes to Christ is declared righteous in God's court of law never to face condemnation for their sins with eternal punishment. Each one becomes a spiritual child of God currently, is forgiven, and destined for eternal fellowship with God, with all believers in Heaven and the new Earth to come.

As I pondered the 29-lesson series of studies used since being at my first incarcerated location, it was laid on my heart to develop a new series of studies that centered on "What is a disciple of Jesus." The Lord has a way of putting things into your mind when he knows you will have the time to conduct the task given. At the time of the prompting, I was not occupied with doing any more book studies, and the correspondence class I was taking from Seminary "Biblical Principles of Interpretation" was almost finished, having only the final exam left. I realized in the middle of all that had occurred, and things that were concluding, that God gave a season of reaping, knowing these men would need discipling, and knowing I would move forward due to Him opening the door. As I prayed for the topics God would have me address in the discipleship studies, I began laying out a list of topics. One after another came to mind, and when I sorted out what the Lord wanted me to develop, the number came to nineteen topical studies. Some of the studies, as they were being written, had two parts and one had three parts which were the continuance of a specific topic. The total of studies came to 25. The twenty-five lesson topics can be reviewed in the Exhibits section.

The following information is primarily for Christians. If you are not a Christian, please turn to the Epilogue, where I give a glimpse of the future, your available opportunity, and offer of eternal security.

I have been troubled by some vital information I requested from my pastor, whom I served under before my imprisonment. I was seeking to know how the overall Christian church is doing in America to fulfill the Great Commission. There are some positives, but overall, there is a regrettable decline. The following was sent to me regarding research taken from Bible.org:

1. Ninety-five percent of all Christians have never won a person to Christ.

2. Eighty percent of all Christians do not consistently witness for Christ.
3. Less than 2% participate in the ministry of evangelism.
4. Seventy-one percent do not give toward the financing of the Great Commission.

The question needing to be asked, "Am I, as a Christian, a part of the statistics which were just given? If so, why?"

Further, George Barna directed the research provided by the American Culture and Faith Institute - ACFI. Before providing the research, some facts proceeded the research which came in the same email:

1. Church attendance is down.
2. Professions of faith are at low levels compared to the past, resulting in a declining percentage of born-again Christians.
3. The number of people who label themselves as Christians is falling. Participation in small groups has dropped by half in less than a decade, as well as adult Sunday school.
4. Bible reading is less common.
5. The number of adults who pray to God has decreased significantly in recent years.

The email stated there is neither an easy explanation nor a single answer to the question of why this is happening. The ACFI states the following about the information just outlined, "Christians are not excited enough about their faith in a relationship with Jesus Christ to share the basics of that faith with non-believers."

And that includes many Bible believing pastors as well.

The ACFI research (in part) is as follows:

* In a nationwide survey of adults, only two out of every ten adults (20%) believe they have a personal responsibility to share their faith in Christ with others who believe differently.
* Among adults, only 23% shared their personal faith monthly during the past year, and many of those who did share their faith either were not Christians or were sharing a version of Christianity that is not biblically grounded.

* In total, ACFI estimates that less than one out of every 10 adults who share a message about their faith with other people at least once a month during the previous year communicated a biblically accurate version of the gospel.

* The survey results among adults suggested that all kinds of divergent ideas about the Christian narrative are conveyed by people to non-believers.

Some examples:

* Among the concepts most likely shared by conservative believers are that people are basically good.
* That some faith is more important than the substance of faith.
* That God exists and is omnipotent and omniscient, but that humankind has evolved from other life forms.
* Eternal security can be assured either through the sacrificial death and resurrection of Christ or by doing enough good deeds to earn God's favor.
* Jesus understands our struggles because He sinned while on Earth.
* Sin is real, but the Holy Spirit and Satan are not.
* ACFI also completed a parallel survey among a national sample of theologically conservative, Protestant pastors. That study revealed that more than one out of every four of them (27%) do not believe they have a personal responsibility to share their faith in Christ, with others who believe differently.

Some positives:

* Denominationally, the survey found that conservative pastors associated with Baptist churches were the most likely to say they have a personal responsibility to evangelize (90%).
* Theologically conservative Protestant pastors were more prone to sharing the gospel. Seventy-one percent of them did so at least once a month during the past year.

* It is estimated there are perhaps 70,000 churches in the U.S. with biblically solid evangelistic pastors.

The research described in the ACFI report is from two surveys conducted in February 2017. One of the surveys is Full View, a monthly national public opinion study. It was conducted online February 1-5, with 1,000 respondents aged 18 or older whose demographic profile reflects that of the United States.

The second survey is the Conservative Clergy Canvass, known as ACFI's C-3 survey. It is, a national public opinion study, which samples 500 clergy, consisting of theologically conservative pastors. It was conducted on-line in February 2017.

One other article was sent to me regarding Millennials. They have been called the social justice generation, due to them actively taking up the cause of the poor, the oppressed, the orphaned and widowed. The Barna research reveals the evangelistic practices of all other generations have either declined or remained static in the past few years. Millennials are the only generation among whom evangelism is significantly on the rise. Their faith-sharing practices have escalated from 56% in 2010 to 65% in 2013. Not only are they involved in the foregoing, but born-again Millennials share their faith more than any other generation today. Nearly 2/3 (65%) presented the gospel to another, within the past year. That is in contrast to the national average of about half (52%) of born-again Christians.

It is a joy to receive the positive stats, regarding sharing the good news of Jesus Christ. The negatives should be alarming to Christians. As I reflected on the statistics, what came to mind was the need for laborers to enter the field of reaching people with the life-saving message of Christ.[22] I began to examine myself, to see where I was regarding reaching others. On occasion, I engaged those at the camp regarding politics, but often neglected speaking about Christ. I remembered Jesus telling his disciples if you love me, keep my commandments, keep my word.[23] Keeping Jesus's word is synonymous with loving Him.

---
[22] Luke 10:2
[23] John 14:15,21,23

I was affected by this as a reminder of what would express my love for my Lord.

The Lord Jesus laid out a strategy to reaching people in need of Him. It is simple, yet profound. There are those across our nation actively doing the work of the Great Commission, but many believers need challenging. I have learned there is biblical precedence of every believer participating in being an instrument in God's hands to reach others with the good news. Jesus called his followers to love each other, our neighbor, and be active in the mission work He assigned. The first, as you are going, share the gospel with those in your world. Secondly, to make disciples of people who have believed from every nationality.[24] Jesus said he would build His church.[25]

But He needs willing followers who will be His voice, hands, and feet. When Jesus called Simon Peter and Andrew, his brother, to follow Him, He told them He would make them become fishers of men (i.e., people).[26] A fisherman is not born a fisherman but is developed and trained to become a fisherman. The same is true with followers of Christ. The people of God can be developed into fishers of people. The task of reaching others with the gospel of peace has been given to every believer. The work is not just for those who have the gift of evangelist. Yet, those gifted in this area are to equip or prepare others in the faith, to do the work of service - (evangelizing).[27] I know this is the area of my calling and focus. The work of service, as related to the evangelist, is to prepare the people of God to do the work of reaching others in their sphere or world of influence, with the gospel message. As a believer is being spiritually matured by one's pastor, as he teaches the word, a sanctifying effect occurs progressively when there is a humble and obedient heart that responds to the Word of God. The evangelist draws alongside to support the work of the pastoral gift, to equip the believer in sharing their faith. The believer must realize for those in their sphere of influence to listen to their witness, he or she should have some evidence of a changing life, which lends credibility to the one sharing the gospel message.

---

[24] Matthew 28:18-20; Mark 16:15
[25] Matthew 16:18
[26] Mark 1:17
[27] Ephesians 4:11-12

The second component is to earn the right to be able to share the plan of salvation with an associate, friend, or family member on a one-to-one basis. Instruction will provide the confidence to move forward in this area, one only must be teachable and willing to learn. Every believer is called to put on the whole armor of God. The principle of "going" is given in the spiritual armor. The principle is given to all believers. My studies have led me to believe each believer is to have their feet covered with the preparation of the gospel of peace.[28] This is the work in which I am engaged. Paul more than likely is relating to the preparedness of the believer, as walking through his or her daily activities having a readiness to engage others with the gospel message. A few other passages related to the believer's feet solidify the principle.

Isaiah 52:7 states as follows, "How beautiful upon the mountains are the feet of him who brings good news, who proclaims peace, who brings glad tidings of good things, who proclaims salvation, who says to Zion, your God reigns." This passage has a double reference both physical and spiritual. In Romans 10:15 it says, "And how shall they preach unless they are sent? As it is written: How beautiful are the feet of those who preach the gospel of peace, who bring glad tidings of good things!"

Every believer is to be involved in this exalted glorious work, which breathes new life into the community of believers. When our Lord spoke to the Ephesian believers concerning the need to do the first works, and if those works were not returned to, He would remove their lampstand (i.e., that community of believers would eventually die out or be discontinued). When local assemblies failed to fulfill the Great Commission of sharing the gospel and making disciples, those assemblies can be diminished or removed as a direct judgment from the Lord Jesus Christ.[29] I can see the judgment across America in the statistics given. I can see the church in many instances has fallen asleep and needs awakening and reviving to the charge given by Christ.

---

[28] Ephesians 6:15
[29] Revelation 2:5

I see the overall Christian church is being distracted with the cares of this world, deceitfulness of riches, and desires for other things – so, the word in one's life is strangled or quenched.[30] The result is the believer is unfruitful in their spiritual growth experience and sharing Christ with others. I am taking a self-evaluation and have determined that I fall short in reaching out to people. I am convinced by the statistics. But I am determined to fulfill God's will for my life, for which I am in pursuit. When my priority is the things above, then all things shall be added to me and any other believer. It is a promise.[31] God knows believers have to earn a living, attend school for educational purposes, and handle household issues. But where does He, our Lord, figure in as related to our reaching our world? The plan is, as we are going…So, who is in my world, as I am going? When I am in the yard, does my neighbor know Christ? At work, does my co-worker know Christ? If I am in school, do my classmates know Christ? When I go on appointments, do those who I meet know Christ? Do my relatives know Christ? Are my children learning about Christ? Who am I conversing with? Jesus is not asking me to go where I am not going. Although, that may come.

There are 168 hours in a week. If I were to take a self-assessment of how I consume my hours, how many hours are devoted to spiritual conversations, or spiritual work? If I aim at nothing spiritually, I will reap nothing practically in a spiritual sense. If I start reordering my time to include growing in the faith and speaking to others regarding the faith, it pleases and honors God and Christ, which brings spiritual dividends, or fruit. God is a fruit inspector. There is no fruit, fruit, more fruit, and much fruit.[32] Bearing fruit glorifies God.[33] These scriptures have been my reminder of the value of reaching people who are so valuable to God being created in His image. In Proverbs 11:30, it states, "The fruit of the righteous is a tree of life, and he who wins souls is wise." In Daniel 12:3, it says, "Those who are wise shall shine like the brightness of the firmament (i.e., sky), and those who turn many to righteousness like the stars forever and ever."

---

[30] Mark 4:19
[31] Matthew 6:33
[32] John 15:2,5
[33] John 15:8

Our Savior, in John 4:35-36, said, "Do you not say, there are still four months and then comes the harvest? Behold, I say to you, lift up your eyes and look at the fields for they are already white for harvest! And he who reaps receives wages, and gathers fruit for eternal life, that both he who sows, and he who reaps may rejoice together."

Over the years I have learned that the Lord elevates the labor of fishing for those in need of Him. All will not come to Christ, I realize that, but it is not that God desires that. Some will even be antagonistic, thinking the message is false. In due time they will discover how wrong they were. I have found the ministry of sharing Christ with the unbelieving world has an incentive. The labor in this area receives wages which are stored up in the believer's spiritual account.[34] The gathering of fruit in the context shared is a picture of people coming to Christ for salvation. The ministry of reaching people with the gospel has brought rejoicing to me for my participation. I have not found a better spiritual legacy that I want to leave in this life, than being an instrument in God's hand, to see others come to Christ, and those who come, fashioned into His disciples to reach others.

God has a call on all our lives, and there is work to be accomplished.

All our Bible training is to develop godly character, and a sound biblical belief system, so we can do the works of service to build up the body of Christ by the power of the Holy Spirit. I can hear some believers saying I do not have the time to participate in reaching others with the gospel. If that is the case, then ask yourself where is all your time going? Will any of us be able to win our case before the Judgment Seat of Christ, when we have to give account for why we could not carry out his plan to reach people in our sphere of influence with the gospel? The answer is obvious. Let us become serious, re-prioritize, make adjustments, and let us follow His will. Remember it is as you are going. Others will say I am afraid to share about my faith in Christ. Paul said he could do all things through Christ, who strengthens me.[35]

---

[34] 2nd Corinthians 1:14; 1st Thessalonians 2:19
[35] Philippians 4:13

The one who is writing this book had fears regarding the call to ministry, due to being one who did not communicate very well, was not very sociable, but more of a quiet reserved person and not very smart in life overall, as shown by my incarceration. I have made a lot of mistakes. One who stumbled over words, but I did not give up, and He said He would never leave me or forsake me. I am sure people thought I was washed up and would never amount to anything, and they were right. However, they did not consider God has a calling for the foolish, the weak, the debased, and the despised.[36] I have heard on several occasions God can take your mess and make it into a message. God can take one further than what one could think and accomplish things that were not imagined if one is humble, faithful, and obedient. My desire above all other desires is to do the will of God and help others do the same because I love Him. God give me the wisdom, courage, and boldness to press on is my prayer. I cannot give God an excuse for not fulfilling my ministry.[37] Jesus dealt with the excuses of His day, and gave an emphatic command in Luke 9:59-60, "Then He said to another, 'Follow Me.' But he said, 'Lord, let me first go and bury my father.' Not that his father had died…It was a stall tactic. Jesus said to him, 'Let the dead bury their own dead, but you go and preach the kingdom of God." The point is the call of God should have priority over everything else. If you are one saying that you are willing to share but do not know how, you can learn.

The Lord wants and needs laborers for the harvest field to reach people in need of Him.

---

[36] 1st Corinthians 1:27-29
[37] Colossians 4:17

Chapter 24

What Now?

As I am nearing the end of this journey of my incarceration, and the end of my book, I hope to stimulate the believing community to participate in the Great Commission. If this is an area you are fully involved in, praise God for your obedience to our Lord's command. If you are not participating in this essential work given to the Christian church, would you consider that the Lord Jesus has a plan for your involvement? There are great Christian ministries across the nation that are evangelical, active in outreach programs of door-to-door witnessing, telephone calling, invite a friend, open-air ministry in parks and stadiums, etc. Some ministries have yearly campaigns, some monthly, or quarterly. Some are successful, and others not so successful. The winning of the unchurched is only the beginning of a process that should have the intent to bring as many as possible to spiritual maturity, which does not happen overnight as many of you know. I believe the church should operate its evangelistic outreach on principle, rather than a program. If the people of God are stimulated and driven by principle rooted in the word of God, it will be the Holy Spirit working to sustain the effort, not the idea of a well-meaning believer. I am not saying ideas are not good, but Holy Spirit driven principles are better. I have already laid the scriptural groundwork that every believer is responsible to carry the gospel to their sphere of influence, (i.e., those in their world). There are ways to enter a spiritual conversation with one who has not come to know Christ in a spiritual relationship. Jesus asked questions, and so can we, to discover if one is interested in having their sins cleansed and receiving forgiveness. There is not a more loving thing that we can do than to alter one's spiritual destiny. If interested, one can learn a set of five questions to open a spiritual conversation and discover if that individual is interested in having the plan of salvation presented to them. The five questions are borrowed, not developed by me, but work in opening a spiritual conversation. I have employed these five questions and have found them very useful. The method does not force your beliefs on one, but rather earns the right to share your faith with them.

I have been using a step-by-step plan that moves a consenting individual through how in the beginning God, and man had a harmonious relationship. This method is also borrowed with a few modifications. It moves the listener through the prohibition God placed upon the first man and woman, and how they were disobedient and caused sin to enter the world. This brought separation between God and themselves. The first two panels address those areas just shared. The third panel walks the listener through the three ways man seeks to reestablish his relationship with God and what the outcome is from their attempt. The fourth panel displays God's only provision in which man can be reunited with Him and why? The fifth and sixth panels lay out the requirements acceptable to God, to embrace the only provision given. All have scriptural support for review. The next panel asks questions to find out if the salvation message is understood. The last two questions ask if the individual has any questions, and the final, if the individual wants to accept the invitation that is offered? If so, the last panel provides a prayer for only the sincere to enter a relationship with the God of creation and salvation through Jesus Christ. Once one prays the prayer of acceptance, the new believer can be shown what the next steps are in the process of growing as a Christian.

The next area of importance is discipleship of the new believer. I believe a very important principle needs embracing by the believing community across the nation. I have been applying the principle by teaching it to the new believers entrusted to me at Mendota camp. I do not know if the terms I will use are already being used in the church from the biblical principle seen in 2 Timothy 2:2. The terms are "Generational Discipleship." The passage is as follows, "And the things that you have heard from me among many witnesses, commit these to faithful people who would be able to teach others also." I use the word people instead of men because in the Greek the word for men is translated Anthropos, which means man-faced, (i.e., male or female). It makes sense, because both men and women are to be involved in making disciples of Jesus Christ. Both men and women, young men and young women are to be involved in spreading the good news of Jesus Christ.

The apostle Paul is speaking to Timothy, his pupil or disciple, whom he mentored in the faith. In this letter Timothy is being instructed to take what he had heard from Paul among many other witnesses and commit those teachings to faithful people. The faithful people are not to keep the teachings to themselves but are to disciple or mentor others. The two requirements are to be faithful and able to teach. The term faithful in Greek is pistos, meaning trustworthy or trustful. Meanwhile, the word able in Greek is hikanos meaning competent or fit (in character), and content (i.e., doctrine). The term teach in Greek is didasko, meaning to give instruction learned. If one does not believe one is a teacher this area can be overcome with the assistance of learning what to teach. I will address this further along. The principle of Generational Discipleship is outlined in the illustration presented below.

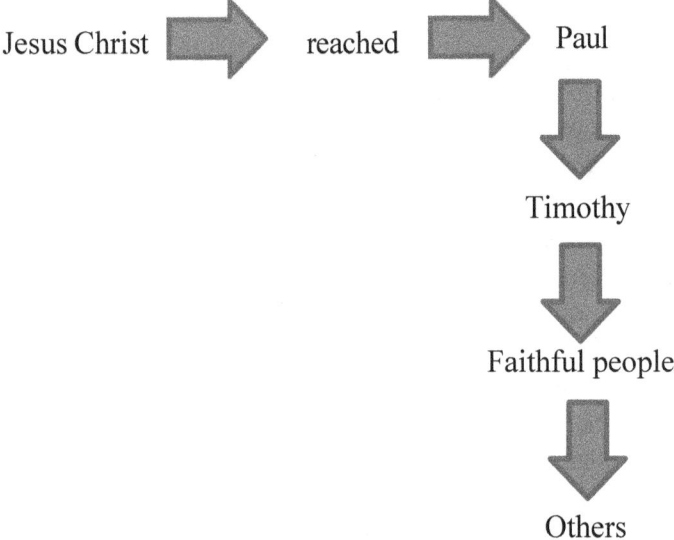

I also have described this as the "Vertical Affect." This biblical model teaches disciples to make disciples who make disciples.

As a reality, many believers for one reason or another will have little interest in one-to-one sharing of their faith, even though the Scripture teaches it.

However, some will respond to the biblical basis of the fact that sharing our faith and making disciples is a part of the work of ministry, to fulfill one's part of the Great Commission. Each believer can reach their sphere of influence (their world of people). Each believer can team up with another believer with a similar interest to pursue the Lord's call.

On the issue of training, I believe the Lord has provided me with teaching materials to assist the believer in discipling and mentoring to their sphere of influence, who respond to the gospel message. The materials have received a very positive response here at Mendota camp. I do not know if the terms I'm using are already being used in the church from the biblical principle seen in 2 Timothy 2:2. The terms again are "Generational Discipleship." I believe it could bring revival to the assemblies across America, not overnight, but progressively. If there is a biblical method your congregation is already employing and it is working satisfactorily, praise God. Those assemblies or individuals wanting to enter dialogue of the discipleship system of studies can contact me. Every believer participating would take ownership of the principle.

What if a congregation of 100 adults, and only 5% respond to the call to share their faith in presenting the gospel? Secondly, these same ones would engage in making disciples, wouldn't that be of worth? The five believers out of the congregation of 100 are provided training, which is the same training for those who respond to Christ. The training would take place over a little more than a year. The same discipleship training materials are used for the respondents to reach their sphere of influence, or the people in their world. In year two, towards year end, three new believers on the average respond to the gospel message by the power of the Holy Spirit and are taken through the discipleship training series. The same effort is replicated in year three and year four. The projections are given below. People are valuable to God and to us, so let us not misconstrue the value of each soul who responds or not. The outline is only a possibility. The visual hypothetical is in the Exhibit section. The following is based on a 100-member congregation with 5% participation.

* If all were to go perfectly, which is unlikely - there are 195 new believers added over four years, almost a 200% increase.

* If half the growth occurs, an additional 98 new believers would almost double the church membership, with a total of 198 believer congregation.

* In this hypothetical model, there is no addition of original members attending the 100 - member church participating in the gospel outreach and making disciples. But what if others are moved to reach out to fulfill their part of the Great Commission?

I have spoken earlier about the plan of salvation which is a part of the overall Generational Discipleship system. Over the years I have been given a three-tier system of biblical studies:

a) The first stage is the "25" lesson initial study resource. The theme throughout is, "What is a disciple of Jesus?" It starts with the assurance of being born again. It is a six-month study, meeting once per week in home or at a desired location. These studies are   question-and-answer   format with   biblical references. Some of the topical studies have quizzes. See Exhibit section for the topical breakdown.

b) The second stage is the 29-lesson topical study resource having questions, answers, and study notes. This is the "We Believe Continued Growth series." The studies are seven months in duration, meeting once per week in home or at a desired location. The frequency of lessons taught per week is at your discretion. See Exhibit section for topics.

c) The third stage is an ongoing 20, New Testament books of in-depth expository verse by verse question and answer study resource, which includes 13 of Paul's epistles and 7 general epistles except for Hebrews. This study group is referred to as Explain Every Verse "EEV" book studies.

These studies are designed to give considerable depth of understanding, which should yield more grounded spiritually mature believers in the faith. The system of studies would assist in developing godly character and training for spiritual warfare. New believers could have a systematic source of studies for continuous activity in the Generational Discipleship process. The study should give more seasoned believers a system of studies that will stimulate further growth and provide a step-by-step system of means to disciple others. The "EEV" book studies are listed in the Exhibit section.

In closing, many believers are following their Earthly stars, for example sports teams, favorite athletes, performing artists, motion picture, and television personalities for entertainment. That is OK. I have areas of enjoyment for relaxation, like you. Most of us may never excel at being a star on Earth from the standpoint of the world, but every believer is given the opportunity to become a star in Heaven by labor in fulfilling our call in the Great Commission, which will last for an eternity. I ask myself what is more valuable to me, being captivated with entertainment surrounding the Earthly stars of this life, or becoming a Heavenly star in the eyes of God in Christ? I have made my choice to participate in the race, run with patience, exerting effort towards reaching others, so they too can be Heaven bound by turning some to righteousness, and making disciples by the power of the gospel and work of the Holy Spirit. May God's hand be upon your lives to do His will is my prayer and finish the work to which He has called each of us. The Epilogue pertains to the future, one's opportunity, and eternal security.

Epilogue

If you are of another faith, I respect your convictions. I will ask, how certain are you in having a peaceful existence entering the next life? If you are open, please continue to read. If not, thank you for your purchase of my book, and your time in reading it. Love, and peace to you...

For those who are continuing to read, you are in for a ride. I want to share with you some things I have learned over the years studying the Bible. You may ask why am I so passionate about spreading the good news regarding Jesus Christ my Lord? I personally do not want anyone to miss the glorious future God has prepared for those who love Him and want to be with Him. Jesus, before going to the cross to pay for our sins, said to His disciples, "Let not your heart be troubled, you believe in God, believe also in Me. In my Father's house are many dwellings; if it were not so, I would have told you. I go to prepare a place for you. And if I go and prepare a place for you, I will come again and receive you to myself; that where I am, there you may be also."[38] Jesus is mentioning His Father's house referring to the glorious and holy city, the New Jerusalem. The Eternal City is mobile.[39] Yes, this city can fly by the power of God... The measurements of the city located presently in Heaven is approximately 1,500 square miles. Its height is also approximately 1,500 miles. The magnitude of the city is so huge that it has 12 foundations. If placed in America the city would stretch from New York City to Florida to Denver, to Canada. The city is made of pure gold, like transparent glass. Each foundation is made with precious stones, the type of stones is listed. When the glory, or light of God, strikes all the different precious stones the emanating array of colors will transcend any brilliance of colors ever seen. The city will have a great wall of approximately 216 feet in height, there will be three gates on each length of the city North, South, East and West. Each gate will be made of a solid pearl. Twelve angels will be stationed at each gate, one per gate. The street of the city is pure gold, like transparent glass.

---

[38] John 14:1-3
[39] Revelation 21:2-4

Jesus said He is preparing a dwelling place for us in the New Jerusalem for those who become Christians, which will be for eternity.
This is the 'Christians' great hope and expectation.

The details of the city can be read in the last book of the Bible - The Revelation of Jesus Christ - Chapter 21. There are no greater details about Heaven and the afterlife that are credible than contained in the Bible. The city is located in the third Heaven, which Paul the apostle identifies as Paradise.[40] The Lord Jesus also mentioned to the criminal being crucified next to Him who believed saying – "Today you will be with me in Paradise."[41] Jesus knew about the life hereafter, because He said He came down from heaven![42] Jesus' statement identifies Him as being Divine. Jesus existed before the virgin birth. Would you want Jesus to prepare a place in the eternal city, the New Jerusalem, for you? My place is prepared based on His word. The beauty is beyond anything we have ever seen. I hope you do not miss out…

There is coming a period on Earth, that those who are genuinely born-again Christians will escape, called the time of Jacob's trouble.[43] It will be the most horrific period on Earth ever occurring. The signal for the entrance into this time, will be the exiting of those who are born-again Christians, referred to as the catching away or rapture of the Church. Jesus Christ said he would keep us from this time of God's wrath.[44] Jesus is referred to as the Lamb of God, and it is His wrath which will come upon the world for its sins.[45] The Christian who has been born again will escape this period of seven years, by being removed from the Earth. This event of removal of millions of saved people worldwide will bring mass hysteria with officials, more than likely putting a spin on the event, which will be deceptive. I do not want to move into the tragic details of the seven-year tribulation period. I mentioned some of the events in the message by Doug Clark when I was saved. But a satanic world ruler will appear to have the answers and deceive the majority. I am hoping you decide not to reject Christ and not have to experience this awful time.

---

[40] 2nd Corinthians 12:1-4
[41] Luke 23:39-43
[42] John 6:37-38
[43] Jeremiah 30:7; Daniel 12:1
[44] 1st Thessalonians 1:10; 4:15-18; 5:9; Revelation 3:10
[45] Revelation 6:12-17

I will say to those who are not convinced, and will forgo receiving Christ, not to accept the mandate to receive the Antichrist's implant in your forehead, or on your hand in order to buy or sell.[46] Most likely this will be some type of advanced digital computer identification. The consequence for doing so is the loss of your soul in eternal torment.[47] The Bible predicts the future, and please read the passages for yourself. I am sharing the truth out of love and do not want anyone to die without Christ...

I want to share about the kingdom, which Christ will set up after His return to Earth to destroy the Antichrist, false prophet, and bind Satan and his fallen angels.[48] The thousand-year reign of Christ on Earth will occur with the participation of all those who exercise faith in the truth of God's word and faith in Jesus Christ. The Earth will be restored to its pre-curse conditions. Those who survived the tribulation will be judged - they are described as sheep and goats, (using figurative speech). The sheep are the believing ones who assisted the Jews and other people, believing in the Messiah Jesus and His return.[49] The goats are the ones who by their actions, rejected the kingdom message and the ministry to their fellow man. The goats accepted the lies of the Antichrist.

The ones who are identified as sheep are the righteous who will repopulate the Earth in the kingdom reign of Christ. They will still have their sinful-flesh inclination, so Christ with those who were gathered in the catching-away will have to reign with a rod of iron (i.e. by law and order).[50] The goats are the unrighteous who are cursed and are removed to experience everlasting fire, prepared for the devil and his angels.[51] Could I mention something here, I have heard people say, "If I go to Hell, all my friends will be there." Please realize there is no air conditioning in Hell. There will be no ice cubes in refreshing drinks to cool one's thirst. There will not be any partying, no outings, sports, food, sex, or entertainment. The lost souls of people are in agony, screaming, and weeping in pain because of the flames, and paying for their sins never to escape. Why would anyone want to experience Hell?

---

[46] Revelation 13:16-18
[47] Revelation 14:9-11
[48] Matthew 25:41; Revelation 19:11-21; 20:1-3
[49] Matthew 25:31-40
[50] Revelation 2:26-27; 3:20, 21
[51] Matthew 25:41,46

In contrast, with Jesus Christ, I get to worship and serve God, be reunited with Christian family that passed on before me or are with me. I have a dwelling place or home designed specifically for me, by Jesus in the New Jerusalem. I will have a new body with super-human capacity, without sin. I will have the ability to materialize and de-materialize. I will have the ability to fly without wings, and eat heavenly, and delicious foods. I will participate in the holy festivals.

I will hold a position of responsible authority based on the work Christ used me to do while on Earth. I will be involved in space travel, beholding the beauty of the new Heavens and Earth that God creates. I will live for eternity in peace and harmony with God, communicating with Him, His people, and His holy angels. This is what our God extends to all those who come to Him through Jesus Christ. There will be fullness of joy. Glory and praise to God! He is good in providing all of this, and more, when we are so unworthy…

In continuing, realize after the tribulation period, humanity and the geological earth has undergone judgment and needs restoration. The following are characteristics of the 1,000-year reign of Christ with the apostles, Old Testament believers, the church, and tribulation believers having governance over the people groups admitted into this period.

1. The wilderness, wasteland, and desert will blossom as the rose.[52]
2. Waters will burst forth in the wilderness, streams in the desert.[53] This will be done by the Spirit of God.[54]
3. There will be grass with reeds and rushes (i.e., stalks and papyrus).[55]
4. Physical healing will occur - the eyes of the blind shall be opened. The ears of the deaf shall be unstopped, the lame shall leap like a deer, and the tongue of the dumb (those who cannot speak) shall sing.[56]
5. The King of Jerusalem will speak peace - His dominion - shall be from sea to sea, and from the river to the ends of the Earth.[57]

---

[52] Isaiah 35:1
[53] Isaiah 35:6
[54] Isaiah 32:15
[55] Isaiah 35:7
[56] Isaiah 35:5,6
[57] Zechariah 9:9-10

6. Every person will have their own vine and fig tree, which are symbols of peace and prosperity.[58]
7. The wolf will dwell with the lamb, the leopard shall lie down with the young goat, the calf and the young lion, and a little child shall lead them.[59]
8. The cow and the bear shall graze, their young ones shall lie down together, the lion shall eat straw like the ox, the nursing child shall play by the cobra's hole, and the weaned child shall put his hand in the viper's den. They shall not hurt nor destroy in all My holy mountain.[60]
9. For the earth will be full of the knowledge of God as the waters cover the sea.[61]
10. People from the nations will be taught the ways of the God of Jacob to walk in His paths.[62]
11. The Lord - King Jesus will judge many peoples and rebuke strong nations, they will beat their swords into plowshares (i.e., hoes and spears) and into pruning knives, nation shall not lift up sword against nation, neither shall they learn war anymore.[63]

Therefore, there will be peaceful coexistence between all peoples on Earth, under the rule of Jesus Christ and His followers.

There will be peace in the animal kingdom, in stark contrast to what is current. There will be a yearly festival called the feast of Tabernacles, which is during the fall harvest lasting for seven days. It will be held to worship the King and God our Savior by the nations that will be in Jerusalem.[64] There will be numerous celebrations and thanksgiving in the kingdom reign of Christ. I have given a summary overview of the future, not in total, but after which studying the Bible for years, provides. No other sacred writing provides real details.

---

[58] Micah 4:4
[59] Isaiah 11:6
[60] Isaiah 11:7-9a
[61] Isaiah 11:9b
[62] Micah 4:2
[63] Micah 4:3;
[64] Zechariah 14:16

Jesus asked His disciples a major question, which I will also ask. In Matthew 16:13, when Jesus came into the region of Caesarea Philippi, which was located north of the Sea of Galilee, at the base of the Southwest slope of Mount Herman, (you can visit these areas today). Geographically, the ancient city of Damascus, in Syria is approximately thirty-five miles northeast of Caesarea Philippi), the question He asked was, "Who do men say that I, the Son of man, am?" The disciples responded in the following ways. Some say John the Baptist, some Elijah, and others Jeremiah or one of the prophets.

He said to them, "But who do you say that I am?" Simon Peter answered and said, "You are the Christ, the Son of the living God." Jesus answered and said to him, "Blessed are you, Simon Bar-Jonah, for flesh and blood has not revealed this to you, but my Father who is in Heaven."[65] For Peter to say, "the Christ, the Son of the living God," is to declare Jesus is God the Son, the Anointed One, who is virgin born.[66]

I want to provide a few observations from Jesus' question to His disciples. The first is that many people have a pre-supposed idea of who Jesus is, as seen by the responses given to Jesus by His disciples of what people were saying about Him. When asked by Jesus, "Who do you say that I am?" Simon Peter gave the correct answer. Jesus responds by letting Simon Peter know it was not through human means the true identity of Jesus was revealed to him. Jesus says His Father in Heaven gave Simon Peter the spiritual insight. The revealing was supernatural. It is my observation that a presentation on who Jesus truly is will take the Father in Heaven to provide the spiritual insight to the listener.

You, or I, may be wondering why did the Father reveal who Jesus was to Simon Peter? I would say it was the Father's will to reveal who Jesus was. You may ask why was it the Father's will to reveal who Jesus was to Simon Peter, but not the others who assumed or presupposed Jesus was someone else? The foundational error people make is thinking or assuming they know who Jesus is, without investigating for themselves what the Scriptures say about Him.

---

[65] Matthew 16:14-17
[66] Hebrews 1:1-9; Isaiah 7:14; Matthew 1:18-25; John 4:25-26

Jesus said, "This is the will of the Father who sent Me, that of all He has given Me I should lose nothing but shall raise it up at the last day."[67] Jesus said the Father sent Him. The heavenly Father already knows who will be a part of the family of God by Jesus' statement. Jesus said that of each person given to Him, He would not lose one. Jesus said He would raise them up at the last day. This is eternal security for a true believer. This indicated Jesus has the power to raise a person who died, back to life. Jesus raised people back to life in His earthly ministry, with eyewitness testimony.[68] Here again, is the great hope and anticipation of a born-again Christian.

The second error is to have a proud heart which thinks one has the answer as to who Jesus is, which conflicts with the Biblical record. The word of God says God resists the proud but gives grace to the humble.[69]

If one has an open heart towards the Bible, God will open up the understanding of the Bible to that person. If a person has a closed heart to the Bible, the understanding of the Bible, leading one to be saved, will be closed by God to that person. The stakes are very high in either knowing who Jesus is,[70] and responding, or not responding to the good news concerning Him. It is the difference between eternal existence upon physical death for one's soul to depart from this dimension and enter Heaven, or to depart and enter where one does not want to go. There is no reversal once we die, nor will one enter some existence where you can purge your sins. It is too late.

As a final appeal - Jesus Christ loves you so much that He died for you. Who do you know will die for someone who wants to murder you? Jesus did. What other religious founder had insurmountable eye-witness testimony that he or she rose bodily from the tomb? Jesus appeared bodily to over 500 people on one occasion, after His resurrection.[71] Historical evidence is very reliable.

You can, right now where you are, repent (i.e., turn away) from your sins and invite Jesus Christ into your life. You must be sincere and real.

---

[67] John 6:39
[68] Matthew 11:2-5; Mark 5:35-43; John 11:25, 43-45
[69] James 4:6
[70] Romans 9:1-5; 1 John 5:20;
[71] 1 Corinthians 15:6

If you want to receive Jesus as Lord and Savior of your life pray this prayer now:

Heavenly Father, I know I am a sinner. I have dishonored, disrespected, and offended you by my sins. I believe that you sent Jesus Christ, who knew no sin, to bear the penalty of my sins, by His substitutionary death on the cross. I believe that Jesus was buried, so my sinful lifestyle would be buried, and that He was raised from the dead the third day, so I could be raised to newness of life, be forgiven, and made a spiritual child of God. Father, I turn now from my sins, and receive Jesus Christ into my heart, as my personal Savior, and Lord of my life. Thank you for saving me and granting me eternal life. In Jesus name I pray. Amen.

If you embraced Jesus Christ for the first time, and prayed that prayer with a sincere heart. Welcome to the family of God!

Let me, or a believer you know, know that you invited Jesus Christ into your heart and life. May God bless you, and now move forward in your faith by desiring the pure milk of God's word that you may grow spiritually. The way with Jesus is the difficult way, not the easy way, but it's the only way to enter Heaven.[72] You will need assistance. (1st Peter 2:1-3). Go to my website - wdmbooks.org. Please email me...

I also want to thank each one of you for purchasing my story. Love, grace, mercy, and peace to each one of you.

---

[72] Matthew 7:13-14; John 14:6

Exhibits:

I. The 25 Lesson Series "What is a disciple of Jesus"
1. Assurance of being born again.
2. One who recognizes who Jesus is and submits to His word.
3. One who is confident that the Bible is genuinely the word of God - part one.
4. One who is confident that the Bible is genuinely the word of God - part two.
5. A disciple of Jesus commits to following Him above all others.
6. A disciple of Jesus loves and gathers with the family of God.
7. A disciple of Jesus develops an eternal perspective and worldview that will keep him or her focused on scriptural priorities - part one.
8. A disciple of Jesus develops an eternal perspective and worldview that will keep him or her focused on scriptural priorities - part two.
9. A disciple of Jesus reads, studies, meditate on, and memorizes the Word of God to be established in faith and practice.
10. A disciple of Jesus will develop a prayer life to advance the kingdom of God and His will - part one.
11. A disciple of Jesus will develop a prayer life to advance the kingdom of God and His will - part two.
12. A disciple of Jesus recognizes he or she is in a daily spiritual battle with their old sinful nature, the corrupt world, and evil spiritual forces.
13. A disciple of Jesus puts on the armor of God in order to stand against the spiritual opposition - part one.
14. A disciple of Jesus puts on the armor of God in order to stand against the spiritual opposition - part two.
15. A disciple of Jesus puts on the armor of God in order to stand against the spiritual opposition - part three.
16. A disciple of Jesus understands the stages of spiritual growth and endeavors to grow – part one.
17. A disciple of Jesus understands the stages of spiritual growth and endeavors to grow - part two.
18. A disciple of Jesus pursues godly characteristics in order to be transformed.

19. A disciple of Jesus obeys godly leadership and is submissive to those over them.
20. A disciple of Jesus cleanses himself or herself of immoral practices in order to be used in God's service.
21. A disciple of Jesus exercises self-discipline and self-control to honor God and maintain a credible witness of the faith.
22. A disciple of Jesus is a good manager of his time, talent, and financial resources or treasure.
23. A disciple of Jesus works out with other believers any disputes.
24. A disciple Jesus learns how to share his or her faith with others needing his or her Lord and Savior.
    24a. Entering A Spiritual Conversation/ Plan of Salvation? / What Now?
25. A disciple of Jesus will eventually mentor others spiritually, to mentor others.

II. The We Believe Continued Growth - 29 Topical Lessons Series:

The study has four divisions: First Division –
1. The Bible
2. The Triune God
3. Jesus Christ
4. Mankind's Fall
5. Salvation
6. Spirit Baptism
7. Water Baptism
8. Prayer and Fasting

The Second Division –
1. Holiness of Life
2. Spirit Empowerment and Filling
3. Communion
4. The Church
5. Primary Purpose
6. Church Government
7. Spiritual Gifts

The Third Division -
   1. Satan and Angels
   2. Spiritual Authority
   3. Marriage
   4. Civil Government
   5. The Grace of Giving
   6. Existence of Heaven
   7. Existence of Hell

The Fourth Division -
   1. The Rapture of the Church
   2. The Judgment Seat of Christ
   3. The Tribulation
   4. The Second Coming of Christ
   5. The Millennium
   6. The Great White Throne Judgment
   7. The Eternal State

III.   Explain Every Verse (EEV), Expository Book Studies:

- Romans
- 1&2 Corinthians
- Galatians
- Ephesians
- Philippians
- Colossians
- 1&2 Thessalonians
- 1&2 Timothy
- Titus
- Philemon
- James
- 1&2 Peter
- 1,2,3 John
- Jude

IV. The following is what was shared at the Volunteers Banquet.

"Giving honor to God, to our warden, to the staff and to the volunteers; it is an honor to share from the heart of the inmates regarding your service to us. In thinking about a word which would express what we feel every time you visit us, the word "love" comes to mind. I want to share on behalf of the inmates from the word love an acrostic of what each letter in love means to us each time we see you.

The first letter - "L," reminds us of your loyalty - as inmates we are aware that you have family, others who you attend to, responsibilities of life, issues to handle, and yet you continue to be loyal, faithful, and resolute in remembering to visit us here in Mendota.

The second letter - "O," reminds us of your obedience to the God you serve who has laid it on your hearts to visit with us, of which some of us are not able to receive visits, whose family may be a great distance away, but through your obedient devotion to coming, makes us remember there are those on the outside who care about us and are thinking about us. To this we say thank you.

The third letter - "V," reminds us of how valuable you are to each of us. Every visit brings an awareness of the sacrifice and gasoline, the time in preparation to speak to us, the time out of your day that can be spent visiting others that you serve. But you turned aside to come and visit us. Thank you for the value you see in us.

The fourth letter - "E," reminds us of the encouragement you bring to each of us by your presence, by your smile, and the words you impart that strengthen us, support us, gives us courage and hope to endure while we are serving out our time. We again say thank you.

In closing: Every time you come, every time you pray for us, every time you speak to us, it expresses L-O-V-E (love) to us. Thank you for coming.

V.   Here is the three-minute speech for at risk-youth.

Hi, I am Robert

I have a wife of 34 years and two adult daughters. My crime was fraud. When you receive investors' money and you do not return it, it's called fraud. Since I received less than 1% of the overall funds raised, I went to trial, I lost and received 12 years for my crime.

I brought great pain and sorrow to my family. When I broke the news to my wife and daughters, the weeping that occurred, I never want to experience again, I broke their hearts.

My oldest daughter was in college, my youngest was 13 years old. I missed birthdays, graduations, holidays, and most of all my oldest daughter's wedding. I could not walk her down the aisle.

My wife had to find work because she was homeschooling my daughter. The embarrassment I brought upon my family when the story hit the newspaper and the TV coverage, we all wanted to hide. The hurt and resentment I caused; I will never be able to erase.

I put a strain on my family relationships to say the least. The financial pressure and my not being there were overwhelming to my family. I realized my bad decisions brought great consequences which I'll always regret. The worst thing about prison for me is I'm not with my family. When I call home, it hurts because I'm not there. Especially during the holidays - Thanksgiving, Christmas, New Year's, and Easter. I hear the interaction in the background, the catching one another up on what's happening in their lives, the good food being enjoyed, and I'm stuck here. I wish I could turn back the clock and eliminate what was done, but I know that is impossible. So, I spend my time in positive activities, because I never want to experience anything like this again. Thank you for your time.

Generational Discipleship (multiplication hypothetical):

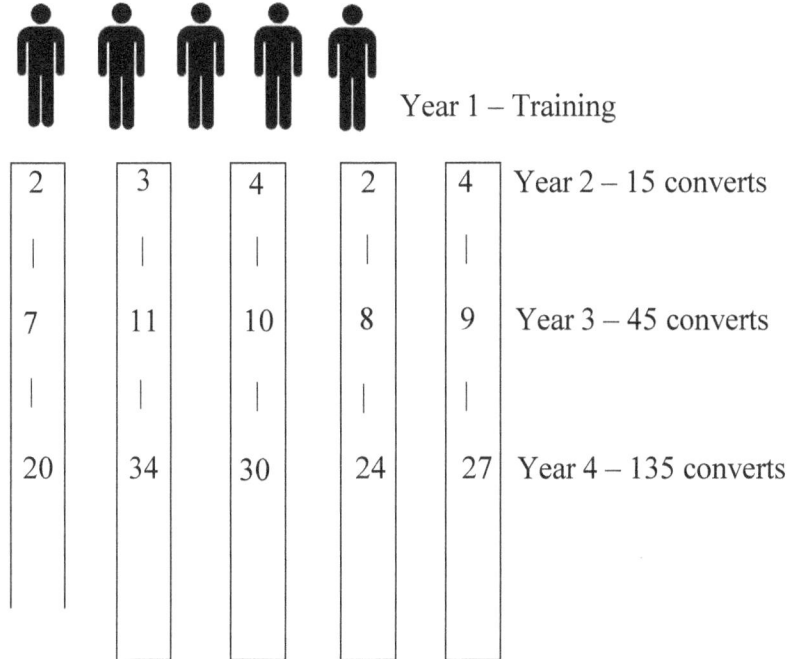

The Believer's Prison Creed

1. Men who are saved can serve King Jesus! Acts 4:10-12
2. Men who love each other serve King Jesus! John 13:34-35
3. Men who read their Bibles and obey it serve King Jesus! Rev. 1:3
4. Men who pray for others serve King Jesus! James 5:16
5. Men who are humble serve King Jesus! James 4:6
6. Men who maintain pure thoughts serve King Jesus! Philippians 4:8-9
7. Men who maintain wholesome speech serve King Jesus! Colossians 3:8
8. Men who guard their eyes and heart from lust serve King Jesus! Matthew 5:28
9. Men who respect others serve King Jesus! Matthew 7:12
10. Men who are givers serve King Jesus! Acts 20: 35
11. Men who confess their sins and forsake them serve King Jesus! Proverbs 28:13
12. Men who pursue godly character serve King Jesus! 2 Timothy 2:22
13. Men who share their faith serve King Jesus! 1 Thessalonians 1:8-10
14. Men who gather for fellowship serve King Jesus! Acts 2:42
15. Men who maintain sexual purity serve King Jesus! 1st Thessalonians 4:3-8
16. Men who aspire to lead a quiet life, mind their own business, and work with their own hands serve King Jesus! 1st Thessalonians 4:11

Men who shunned these things do not serve King Jesus *

Reference Credits

i. Information taken from Los Angeles County (.gov) > parks.
ii. The information was taken from Wikipedia, Watts Neighborhood Council.
iii. The facts on anthracite coal are taken from the New Encyclopedia Britannica 2010
iv. Taken from Social Solutions (SS)

Location Maps

Location Map #1
Guadalajara, Jalisco, Mexico Cancún, Mexico

Location Map #2

St. Thomas & St John, U.S., Virgin Islands; Grand Cayman Island; Cozumel; Dominican Republic

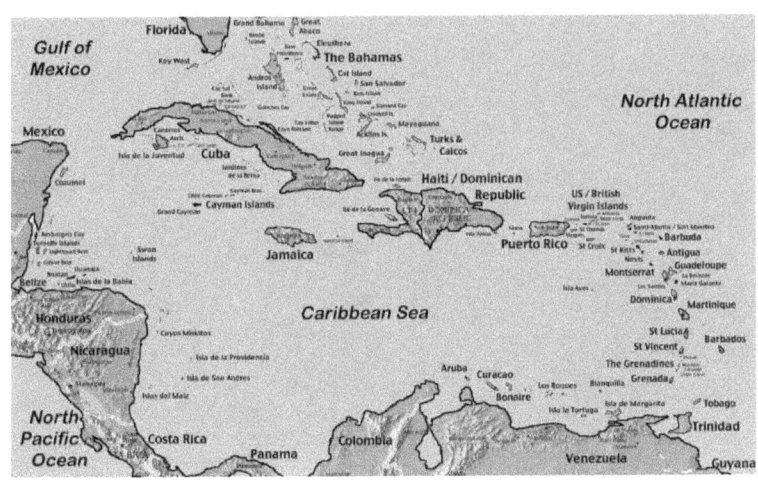

Location Map #3
Kauai, Hawaii

Location Map #4

Ho Chi Minh City, Vietnam; Hanoi, Vietnam; Beijing, China; Taipei, Taiwan

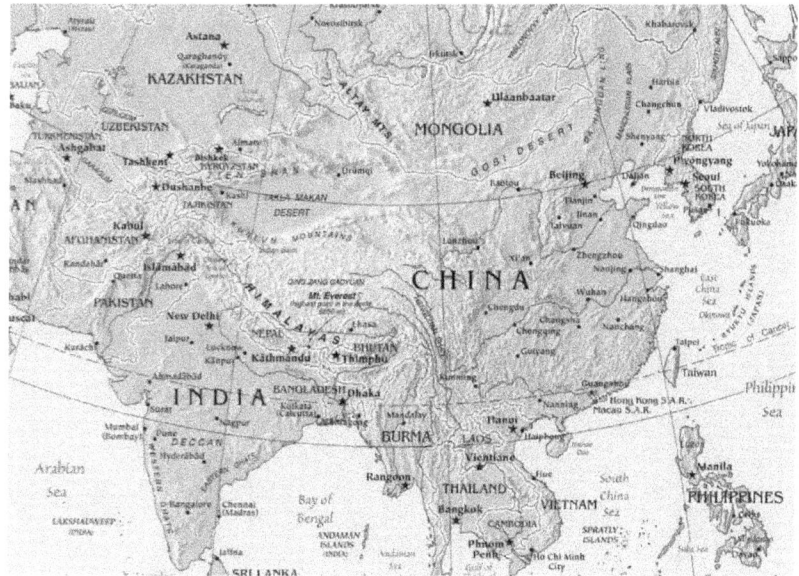

Location Map #5

Liechtenstein

www.ingramcontent.com/pod-product-compliance
Lightning Source LLC
Chambersburg PA
CBHW020542030426
42337CB00013B/944